IN SURE AND CERTAIN HOPE

An Anthology of Exemplary Funeral Messages

IN SURE AND CERTAIN HOPE

3.86 2T

6803 / ISBN 0-89536-785-8   PRINTED IN U.S.A.

Table of Contents

74057

Part 1. Preaching on Death at Sunday Worship

Standing Up To Death

Psalm 90
Romans 6
1 Corinthians 15

If it has not happened to you yet, you can be sure that sooner or later life is going to acquaint you with death. We can decide whether or not we want to go to Australia; we have the option of eating horsemeat or not eating horsemeat; but we do not have the option of meeting death or not meeting death. We will meet it, perhaps have already met it, of this we can be sure.

But meeting it does not mean that we automatically have made our peace with it. Meeting it does not mean that we have accepted it, befriended it, integrated its reality into our lives. Young people are listening to a song these days that carries the line, "I'm going to live forever." It's repeated many times in the song and maybe some hear that so often they begin to believe they will never have to die.

I realize this isn't a pleasant subject, but it is an important one. Failing to come to grips with it now can mean setting ourselves up for much unhappiness later. Where are you in the process of accepting death — your death and the death of people who are close to you?

A way of answering that question for ourselves is to answer for ourselves other questions. Questions like these:

When people around me begin to talk about death, do I find myself changing the subject?

When I talk about the death of other people, do I find myself employing euphemisms? Do I say that John "passed away" or "has left us" or "has gone onto his reward" instead of saying "John died"? In thinking of my own death, do I couch it in terms like, "If anything should ever happen to me?"

Have I taken steps to make sure that my house is legally in order? Have I, for example, made out a will?

With regard to final arrangements, does someone else know what my preferences are — what kind of service I want, what I want done with my body, how much money I prefer to spend?

I raise these issues not to start your day off on a sour note, but rather to remind you that our Christian faith is not silent on this matter of death. It stands ready to help us and it helps us concretely in the following ways.

Death is Natural

The Christian faith reminds us of the Biblical truth that death is natural. It is not an alien intruder coming to bring something that, under normal conditions, would not be in the picture. It is not a spoilsport. Death is a reality we share with all of the created order. The Old Testament speaks of a man "full of years" being "gathered to his people."

Psalm 90 relates the naturalness of death too —

Thou turnest man back into dust;
"Turn back," thou sayest, "you sons of men;"
for in thy sight a thousand years are as yesterday;
a night-watch passes, and thou hast cut them off;
they are like a dream at daybreak,
they fade like grass which springs up with the morning
but when evening comes is parched and withered.

To employ a phrase from St. Paul, as human beings we bear "the image of the man of dust." Our organic systems, bionics notwithstanding, were intended to come to a point of zenith and then decline.

This naturalness is conveyed, I think, in a bit of dialogue from Margaret Craven's book *I Heard the Owl Call My Name.* It is the story of a young vicar, serving the Indians of the Northwest, who faces an early death. At one point this young vicar and his bishop are returning to civilization and when they reach an inlet, this interchange ensues:

When they entered the inlet, the Bishop motioned Mark to stop the engine.

"Let's not hurry," he said. "It's so seldom I have a few hours to myself."

The breeze was gentle with the first promise of spring. They could see the float moored to the inlet side and beyond it they could see the jagged scar of the great slide.

"Always when I leave the village," the Bishop said slowly, "I try to define what it means to me, why it sends me back to the world refreshed and confident. Always I fail. It is so simple, it is difficult. When I try to put it into words, it comes out one of those unctuous, over-pious platitudes at which Bishops are expected to excel."

They both laughed.

"But when I reach here and see the great scar where the inlet side shows its bones, for a moment I know."

"Why, my lord?"

"That for me it has always been easier here, where only the fundamentals count, to learn what every man must learn in this world."

"And that, my lord?"

"Enough of the meaning of life to be ready to die," and the Bishop motioned Mark to start the motor, and they went on.

To be ready to die at the end of life is as natural as being ready to grab hold of life at its beginning. It is this lesson that older people can and do teach us. I've talked to a countless number of people in the afternoon of life who have said to me that they are ready to die, not afraid to die, open to death and I am reassured by their feelings and expressions.

Death as the Absence of Quality Life

But the scope of death is infinitely greater than its dominion over our bodies. And that dominion is both negative and positive.

It's positive in the sense that some parts of our lives have to die so that other parts can be born into their fullness. A family, which has been two, dies to its twoness so that it can become a threesome. A minister dies to one parish so that he can be born to another and well I remember the dreams of death in Boston as we prepared to move to Glens Falls. A person dies to her vocation in later life so that she can be born into the delights of life's late afternoon. Although the text has been victimized by those whose faith has soured and become dogma, the New Testament reminds us that we "must be born again." Indeed, our faith sometimes has to die (and we call that death of faith *doubt*), so that a deeper and more viable faith can be born (and we call that birth *conversion*). "Death appears in order to make way for transformation," writes James Hillman, and each day we are in the process of becoming more whole and more human. Here the contribution of death is positive.

There is a line from Bernard Malamud's novel, *God's Grace*, where God declares: "From the beginning, when I gave them the gift of life, they were perversely greedy for death." This points to death's negative dominion over life.

We've seen enough television and watched enough films to have in mind the procedure a doctor follows when he is examining a person to see if physical death has occurred. The doctor feels for the pulse and listens for the heart. It's all rather cut and dried, although with the development of medical technology and its ability to artificially sustain life, a gray area has evolved. Still, the signs are fairly obvious.

The New Testament suggests there is an obviousness about the death of the inner person. And the sixth chapter of Romans spells the reality of this death right out. A few sample lines will make this clear —

> *"Do you not know that all of us who have been baptized into Christ Jesus were baptized into his death? We were buried therefore with him by baptism into death, so that as Christ was raised from the dead by the glory of the Father, we too might walk in newness of life." (Romans 6:3-4)*

> *"So you must consider yourselves dead to sin and alive to God in Jesus Christ." (Romans 6:11)*

> *"For the wages of sin is death, but the free gift of God is eternal life in Christ Jesus our Lord."*

It is wholly possible for a person to be, organically speaking, disease-free and be dead on a far more insidious basis. The living dead, we sometimes call them. You've seen them, and I've seen them. The New Testament calls them people captured by sin. To use that word is to open a can of worms because there are always folk who want to particularize it and label this particular act sin and that particular act sin, resulting in a version of Christian life not unlike that childish game of walking the sidewalks, but not stepping on the cracks. The Bible, particularly the New Testament, has a more comprehensive understanding of the word. Paul reminds us that all have sinned and fallen short of God's glory. Sin, according to the New Testament, is more condition than act and fundamentally it means separation from God and God's purposes. It is separation from God and God's grace that is the hallmark of the living dead. A list of the living dead might include the following:

> *Those preoccupied with a perfection that is beyond human reach.*
> *Those whose energies are kidnapped by and now serve the forces of an inordinate guilt.*
> *Those whose relational ways are the ways of manipulation.*
> *Those who place economic gain over human welfare.*
> *Those who think far too little of themselves and carry an imaginary sign over their heads that reads, "Unworthy, unworthy."*
> *Those who think too much of themselves and adopt patterns of condescension.*

You can probably call to mind individuals you know who are dead on this basis. The Bible, too, is full of people like this. But it is also the story of God rescuing people from the jaws of this death.

As we talk together about this, the imagery of a massive jail comes to my mind and in this jail there are many cellblocks, with each of these cellblocks containing many small cells. People like you and me populate those cells — cells of separation, loneliness, moral failure, depression and fear; cells of death. Suddenly God comes through the front door of this massive jail and in God's hand is a ring of keys. God is running from cellblock to cellblock, opening all these cell doors and as he does so, He is imploring people to come out. "Come out of there," God is saying, "You've been in there for far too long. You are mine and I need you in my kingdom building. Your sins are forgiven. Come out into the light of my day and into the warmth of my presence. Together we have work to do and without you, my efforts will be less than they can be with you. Stand up! Gather up your belongings! Follow me — out the front door and into the light of my kingdom!"

Standing Up To Death

Finally, the Christian faith helps us because it stands up to death.

In death's presence, physical or spiritual, it does not cower or crawl or beg or whine or squirm. To the contrary, our faith says — eyeball to eyeball with death —

"O death, where is thy victory?
O death, where is thy sting?"

I know from the experience of my own life that God can call us from the death of an unfulfilling life. Furthermore, I can't begin to tell you how many times I have stood at the edge of a grave for a committal service. What happens there seems far removed from the central thrust of Christian affirmation. The action really isn't there — near the grave nor in the grave. The action is with God and God's raising of his children.

That this is so will never be proven on the basis of scientific evidence. How could it be? To try and prove the resurrection in the same sense that the scientist proves her theory or that the mathematician proves his theorem makes as much sense as the scientist or the mathematician trying to prove that someone is in love; it's like trying to build a house with a sewing machine: the tool is inappropriate to the job! The scientist, on the basis of scientific procedure, ascertains scientific veracity. But the soul also knows what the soul knows.

The other night I had a dream of my mother-in-law. Mother has been physically gone for over three years now, but it is the verdict of my unconscious that mother is not gone. The church affirms the communion of the saints. That my mind can neither prove nor disprove. But my heart and my soul do not really care what my mind believes or not. They know what they believe.

The Christian faith helps us stand up to death. It looks death in the eye and says, "Death, you have been overrated; your power has been overestimated; your influence has been miscalculated. Some influence you have, but much that people have led us to believe you can do you cannot. You can't squelch my ultimate identity; you can't destroy what is essentially me; you can't kidnap me from God. From you I will not run. Do to me what is yours to do, because you will not be my undoing. Death, where is your victory? Grave, where is your sting?"

Part 2. Funeral Preaching in a General Context

God's Everlasting Love

Romans 8:31-39

Each one of us must face the realities of life everyday. Today, however, in a special way, we face the reality of death. Death is truly a strong power. It can separate us from loved ones, it can bring moments of loneliness for those who survive, it can make us call into question all that we believe. Today we are faced with the death of one whom we loved. I'm sure many of you have already thought ahead to moments of loneliness you will face. Yes, death is real, death is powerful.

But that is not the end of the story today. If it were, there would be no reason for us to be gathered here together. We are here because we realize: death, with all of its power, can be overcome; our Lord and Savior, Jesus Christ, overcame the grave that we might have life, whoever calls upon his name might live.

Earlier, one of my favorite Bible passages was read, Romans 8:31-39. Think on these words again. "I am sure that neither death, nor life, nor angels, nor principalities, nor things present, nor things to come, nor powers, nor height, nor depth, nor anything else in all creation will be able to separate us from the love of God in Christ Jesus our Lord." Nothing separates us from God and his Love! What a glorious promise! It turns death in all its reality, into a beautiful thing.

One of the most beautiful and peaceful sights I have ever seen occurred during a January snowstorm. As I was driving down the street I passed a cemetery and all of the graves and stones were covered with a blanket of fresh, white snow. I couldn't help but think of how in the same manner Christ overcame death, and turned it into something beautiful, the hope of the resurrection.

We often think of the American people as the most advanced people on earth, and in some ways this is true. After all, we have been able to send men to the moon and back. In other ways, however, there is much we can and should learn from our neighbors in other countries. In many ways they have a less cluttered understanding of life and death. For instance, when someone dies, we normally say something like, "He has departed," or "He has left us." Christians in Africa, when talking of the death of a loved one say, "He has arrived," "He has reached his destination." What a beautiful thought! For the Christian, death is not the end of life, it is the beginning. It is the beginning of new life, in a much more glorious way than we have ever before experienced.

There is grief felt by all of us today, and rightly so, but we must remember that this grief is for ourselves. There is an emptiness in our lives and we feel sad. But along with our tears of sadness, we also have tears of joy. Joy in the sure and certain hope of the Resurrection. In the Resurrection, the world of the finite becomes the glorious eternal, anxiety becomes peace, loss becomes hope. These changes can only take place in the presence of Christ. In him we find eternity, in him we find peace, in him we find hope. Through Christ, meaning and strength flow. Meaning to understand, and strength to face tomorrow.

In the Gospel of John our Lord said, "I am the Way, the Truth, and the Life." What comfort in these words! It is through the Lord, that we know the way of salvation. It is in him that we see the Truth, and it is with him that we have the assurance of Everlasting Life. He is the one whom we follow, he is the light which shines on in the darkness, and overcomes that darkness.

As I was preparing this message for today, I couldn't help but think of the story of the father who went with his son one day to visit a nearby town. This was in the days when you walked everywhere, and along the way the two had to cross a weak, old bridge. Once on the bridge, the son was frightened as he looked at the swirling water below. He worried all day because he knew they had to come back the same way and by then it would be dark. It was late in the afternoon when they started to return home. The father sensed that his son was nervous, so he picked him up and carried him. Soon the boy was fast asleep. When he awakened he was surprised to find he was home, it was morning, and the sun was shining brightly. With his father he had gone safely on his way. And so it is at the end of life. There is nothing to fear as long as we know that we are in the presence of him who has power over life and power over death. In this hope we may live, for we know we shall be with God. Today, this is his promise. Today, this is reality.

And now it is up to us to proclaim, in all that we say and do, this "Good News" of God's presence in our lives. May the reality of his love strengthen you today and may you be assured that nothing can separate you from his Everlasting Love.

Part 3. Funeral Sermons for Life-long Christians

A Christian Example

1 Corinthians 11:1

*This is a funeral sermon for a retired minister who lived
in our neighborhood and continued to serve the Lord in
a quiet, unobtrusive manner. He was a genuine saint of
God — faithful, humble, talented, effective. When he
died at the age of almost ninety, the entire community
mourned. It is much more personal and individual than
my typical funeral sermon. Such an occasion lends itself
to this approach.*

As we gather for this Memorial Service for Dr. _____
we have no regret — except the sadness we experience because of
the loss we have suffered. We shall greatly miss him. Our tears of
grief are for ourselves, not him.

Let me encourage you to separate yourself, as far as is possible,
from the present and look backward into the past, there recalling
your personal and joyful experiences with Dr. _____.

Then let me encourage you to look in the other direction — forward into the future, with our Christian assurance of eternal life on
the other side of death.

If you can think of the past, with its happy memories, and of the future, with its hope of reunion, this will greatly help you in living through this present moment of sadness.

Dr. _____, a dedicated Christian minister, has served the Lord for a long while — almost seventy years. He "retired" (supposedly) before I was graduated from seminary.

It is fitting that he should be called home so soon following the passing of his good wife. After almost sixty years together here, they are now reunited, after just a brief separation.

Mrs. _____ left us just two weeks before Christmas. Now, just two weeks following Easter, he has gone to join her. Is it merely a coincidence that their deaths span the life of the Saviour they each served so faithfully!

Let me remind you of some of the things I remember concerning Dr. _____:

1. His great sense of humor. One memory of him is that of a man who always wore a smile, was ever ready with a quick joke or story, whose personality was everlastingly happy and joyful.

2. His love of children. All the children of this church knew Dr._____. And they returned the love they found in his association with them. His special "handshake" (a unique way of using the little fingers) is something that these children will always remember. For a man of his age, his oneness with the new generation was unique.

3. His comfort to the sick and the sorrowing. His retirement was only official in the records. As a matter of every-day living, he was active and concerned. And one of his basic considerations was for those who were enduring the burdensome and pressing experiences of life. He did much visiting — especially in the hospitals and in the homes of our shut-in and elderly persons.

4. His preaching ability. As a preacher, he was one of the finest. He enjoyed attending the seassions of the Annual Conference and was present for sixty-three consecutive roll-calls. He was held in high esteem by his fellow-ministers, and was selected by them for high positions: Conference Secretary, Executive Secretary of the Pension Fund, District Superintendent, delegate to General Conference, etc. And he proclaimed the Gospel right to the end — just last summer, while I was away for a vacation, he supplied this pulpit.

5. His teaching talent. How thoroughly he enjoyed the opportunity to open up the Scriptures and apply them to the contemporary

world. He continued, week after week, teaching an Adult Class which appreciated the study and effort he put into his preparation — until just last month.

Dr. _____ had a sense of humor and a love for children; he was a comfort to the sick and sorrowing; he was a preacher and a teacher. And how true it is that Jesus was also all these things. Yes, Jesus demonstrated these characteristics — and wants his disciples today to practice these qualities.

Paul said, "Be ye followers of me, even as I also am of Christ" (1 Corinthians 11:1). I thoroughly believe that Dr. _____ could have made the same statement. Let us seek to follow this example.

This room is flooded with music. I do not mean the sound of the organ, which we heard played so beautifully just a short time ago. Right at this very moment, music fills this sanctuary. We hear it not, but if we had a small box, plugged into an electric outlet, and were tuned in at the proper wave length, our radio would bring us the music which is in the air surrounding us.

So it is that this room is flooded with the presence of God. If we are not aware of it, 'tis only because our souls are not tuned in on the proper spiritual wave length. Tune in now, by faith, and allow the Lord, whom Dr. _____ followed, to speak his words of comfort, guidance, strength, and challenge.

For a seventy-year-old woman   *Lawrence Ruegg*

A Living Sacrifice

Romans 12:1-2

*This funeral sermon was for a woman who had been a
faithful member of the church most of her life — a person who put her faith into practice at every hour and situation.*

"Therefore, I appeal to you, brethren, by the mercies of God
to present your bodies as a living sacrifice, holy and acceptable to
God; which is your spiritual worship. Do not be conformed to this
world but be transformed by the renewal of your mind, that you
may prove what is the will of God, what is good and acceptable and
perfect."

In the calendar of the Church Year, one day is set aside to com-
memorate St. Augustine. There is much that could be said about
him; but of greater significance today is his mother, Monica, who
for years had hoped and prayed that her son would become a Christian. His mother kept on hoping, praying, believing; until one day
Augustine had a religious conversion and was finally baptized at age
thirty-three in the presence of his mother. St. Augustine, himself,
attributes much of his conversion experience to the faithfulness and
the prayers of his mother. The Bible speaks about the sins of the

fathers being visited upon their children; but it was Charles Dickens who wrote: "I think it must somewhere be written that the virtues of mothers shall be visited on their children, as well as the sins of their fathers."

St. Paul writes to all Christians through his letter to the Christians at Rome. It is interesting to note that Paul expounded for eleven chapters in that book about what God has done for us in the life and sacrifice and resurrection of Jesus the Christ. And then Paul used the last five chapters to speak about our response to God's Grace in his forgiveness and salvation. Chapter twelve begins the transition between what God has done for us and what we can now do in the name of God: and it begins with the word "therefore." "THEREFORE" — because of all that God has done for you — "Therefore I appeal to you to present your bodies as a living sacrifice . . . that you may prove what is the will of God, what is good and acceptable and perfect."

You may think that the initials of _____ are [A, B, C]. If that were the only truth, then there is little that we could celebrate today: "God gave; God took away; and somehow we must bless the name of God." I am here to testify to those who may not really have known her; and also to remind those of you who knew her so well, that _____ had other initials; and it is because of that something extra that the sorrow of her exit from this life cannot equal the joy and comfort that having lived in her shadow brings.

I want to bear witness that she had other initials. Three of them were L.C.W. Yes, I know they stand for Lutheran Church Women; but they signify something far greater than that. They remind me that today we bury the body — not the person — the body of a Church Woman; a Christian, whose first values related to the Lord of the Church. L.C.W. is a symbol of that; and many of you know how great her love was for that organization, because her greater love was for her Lord and Savior, Jesus.

In the life of this modern saint — and in her suffering and dying — the initials L.C.W. remind me of all that Paul has written about in the first eleven chapters of Romans. Her faith was not the result of her good works. Her faith was a gift of God, acknowledged often by her with deep gratitude and thanksgiving. She was dedicated to that Gospel of God; that Good News that life is meaningful and eternal only in the death and resurrection of God's Son.

But there is another set of initials which describe her; initials which grow out of the first; initials which relate to the second section of Paul's letter to Christians at Rome. "Therefore I appeal to you to present your bodies as a living sacrifice . . . that you may prove what is the will of God, what is good and acceptable and perfect."

How do you spell that? Well, people can spell in it many different ways because we are all different people. But in _____ case it is spelled: R.S.V.P.: Retired Senior Volunteer Program. And many of you here know of her great love and dedication to those initials.

Here is Christian response: here is the response of a Christian to all that God has done for us in our salvation. We call these works good because they are done for others out of the goodness which God has done for us. I think _____ own words can best state it. She wrote: "When I was asked to witness about my God-given time, I had to admit that I waste much of it, just as we all do. However, there are a few ways that I use it I want to share with you.

"Talking to people I know and some I don't know wherever I meet them; remembering to keep your tears to yourself but sharing your courage and in some way let them know of God's reassuring love. There are many lonely people in a world today. A few minutes talking with them doesn't cost a cent. Another way I use my time is sending a note or card to someone in trouble, ill, or perhaps full of joy. Again, it lets them know you want to share God's love with them and that you care.

"Then, I find prayer takes much of my time; not long, formal, memorized prayers, but a sort of lengthy conversation with my Lord, thanking him for my many blessings, asking him for guidance in what I say and do; asking him for hope and comfort for others; asking him for forgiveness; praying that with his help I may be able to fulfill his purpose for each new day he gives me; praying that I might be still and listen to what he is trying to tell me. And so it goes throughout my day of time."

St. Augustine's mother died shortly after his baptism. Another mother has died. But who are the real saints: Paul? Augustine? Monica? _____? We are all saints in Jesus Christ. And that is what makes this a day of celebration. Christ rose from death and all who live and believe in him never die; only their bodies die and that is all that we return to the earth.

The sorrow of her death cannot match the peace of knowing who she is and where she now is. The loneliness that her death brings cannot equal the comfort that comes from the presence of the God whom she so faithfully followed. The guilt that one's death opens up to us all is covered and removed by the loving forgiveness from the One God who both welcomes her into his Heaven and reassures us on this earth.

What more can we say? We pray for God's love upon us and we commend to God one whose initials are L.C.W., praise of God, and R.S.V.P., service to people, and whose name is _____; who has indeed presented herself as a living sacrifice and proved what is the will of God, and what is good and acceptable and perfect.

"Well done, thou good and faithful servant."

Amen.

Part 4. Funeral Preaching at Special Seasons of the Year

Buried and Risen With Christ

Romans 6:3-4

This was a funeral meditation for the oldest member of St. John's Lutheran Church, Cherryville, North Carolina, held on Good Friday.

Last evening the Maundy Thursday service concluded with the dramatic act known as Stripping of the Altar. The candles were extinguished. All the rich symbolism here in the chancel was removed: the banners, the Bible markers from the lectern and pulpit, flowers, candles, torches, communion trays, paraments. This black cross was brought in and placed where you see it now.

Last evening we prepared for a death — the death of Jesus of Nazareth. He was crucified on a rise outside the walls of Jerusalem nearly 2,000 years ago. When the Worship and Music committee made plans for our services on Maundy Thursday and Good Friday, the committee was unaware of course that we would be holding a burial service on Good Friday for our oldest member here at St. John's. _____ lived a glorious span of ninety-six years.

But how appropriate is this service on this day. The remark was made to me, "I can't think of a better time for a funeral than Good Friday." As St. Paul said in Romans 6:3-4 "Do you not know that all of us who have been baptized into Christ Jesus were baptized into his death? We were buried therefore with him by baptism into death, so that as Christ was raised from the dead by the glory of the Father, we too might walk in newness of life."

This day has been known through the centuries by two names: Black Friday and Good Friday. Both elements are present.

It is a black day when death occurs, especially the death of the sinless Son of God at the hands of sinful men. Our symbolism for this day undergirds the blackness of this event. All the rich symbolism is removed. The light of candles is extinguished. And the cross is draped in black. Death is the final enemy to be overcome.

But how grateful we are that this is also Good Friday. Death has been conquered. The sting of death and sin is removed. Easter looms just over the horizon. Soon the gloom of death will be replaced with the joy of life. The candles will be lit again. Flowers will adorn the altar. The white paraments of life and joy will be in place. Lilies will witness to the resurrection of Jesus. And this black cross will be bedecked with a rainbow of garden flowers. What a transformation will occur between Good Friday and Easter.

Yes, this is Good Friday too. Black Friday because of the sinfulness of man, what we have done to Jesus. But Good Friday because of what God has done for us in Christ. "As in Adam all die, so also in Christ shall all be made alive."

After his retirement, _____ took care of the cemetery here at St. John's. He cut the grass and kept it presentable. A cemetery will now be his final earthly resting place just as a tomb was the final earthly resting place for Jesus.

_____ will be buried with Christ on Good Friday. But what a transformation we look forward to. He will rise with him in the resurrection. "Death is swallowed up in victory." "The sting of death is sin, and the power of sin is the law. But thanks be to God, who gives us the victory through our Lord Jesus Christ."

Amen.

A Sermon Preached at Christmastime   *Daniel M. Shutters*

Expectations of Hope

John 12:24-26

*_____ death from melanoma occurred when he
was thirty-eight years old. The early December death was
marked by periods of hope and despair, but most assur-
edly by faith.*

It is a time of joy and sadness. The joy of the approaching Christmas season fades into darkness as we experience death in our midst.
The scripture passages we read from the Gospel echo Christ's entry
into Jerusalem for the celebration which leads to the crucifixion of
Christ. The progress and setbacks of _____ illness are
paralleled in the events we recognize later in the Spring of the Church
Year . . . The Sunday of the Passion began so full of hope, laughter, shouts and smiles of anticipation and expectation.

Each year we begin anew the cycle of liturgy which follows the
life of Christ. We start with Advent, the preparation for the coming
of the birth of Christ. We move into the Epiphany Season — that
time which celebrates the manifestation of Christ. We listen in those
days as the Gospel speaks of the miracles that Christ performed.
Quickly, we move into Lent, and the warnings of the crucifixion are
all around us, but the Sunday of the Passion gives us reason to hope

again, only to have the week end, with the Good Friday crucifixion of Christ. Liturgically we move through the life of Christ, between now and Good Friday.

As we read the Scriptures in these coming months we note the rays of hope in the life of Christ. The Gospels speak to us of high hopes when the three magi sought him out. More words of joy are discovered when it was first found that Christ had within himself the power to heal, to alleviate suffering, to raise Lazarus from the dead. There must have been high hopes for the people who were around him then. Just to listen to the teachings of Christ — the parables and sermons — must have given encouragement to many in those days.

But the thirty-three year progress of life also contained seeds of an adverse nature. There was bad news as well as good news, and the bad came to outshadow the good. With our hindsight we can see how the seeds grew. From the very beginning of his life on earth, Herod was there hunting Jesus down. The scribes, the lawyers of the day challenged Christ, setting traps for him. The evil force which tempted him as he began his ministry, showed itself again at the end. And the seeds grew and seemed to choke out the wonderful hope and promise that was in the beginning. If we had been privy to the fateful undercurrent, we would not have been as elated as the disciples who shared in that last supper, with Christ, because a betrayal was taking place. The fruit of those early seeds began to ripen and it led to a quick death for Christ on the cross.

He died, and what are we left with? Questions and memories. The primary question which occurs, as we witness one of our own passing away from our care, is why? Why does God permit pain and suffering, disease and death to take place? Doubts plague us about this God who permits such suffering to take place. But the cause of disease, death and suffering is not God. It is you and I. We are responsible for the bickering, the war, the hatred, the pollution which is inflicted on our lives. The story is told of a man who questioned God saying, "Lord, why do you permit this sickness to take place?" God answered, "Man, I gave you a cure for that illness. I planted the seeds of the idea in the minds of one of your own people." And the man said, "Where is that person? Why hasn't he come forward yet with the cure?" To which the Lord responded, "You killed him. One of your people ran his car over him while driving in a drunken state before he was even ten years old." We are the ones responsible for the ills that have befallen us.

The Lord gives us the tools and we abuse them; we don't use them. Mankind is the one who causes most of the suffering, the war, and the death with which we are surrounded. God, if you will remember, is the one who was willing to suffer for us. God was the one who was willing to take the pain on himself. He sent his Son, Jesus, to be the Christ, to become one of us and to take on the pains of mankind. He gave his son to be crucified. We do not worship two Gods — one who is evil and one who is good. This is one Lord. It is incongruous for there to be two Gods, two natures wrapped up in this one. One who enjoys the inflicting of pain and the other who is willing to suffer himself upon the cross for our sake. How many of you, as parents, would inflict pain upon your children? How many of you would give your child a stone when he asks for bread? None, I surmise, and neither would the Lord God.

Because of God's son, we are heirs of one great gift — hope. Hope which renews itself as we retell the old, old story. As we participate in the Lord's Supper, we have hope. As we remember the Christ who suffered for us that we might not suffer the ultimate death, we have hope. But most emphatically we remember the resurrection of life, and we have hope.

The end of Christ's life, the end of our life, of _____ life, has an epilogue. The final chapter is not death, not the grain cut in full bloom when it is harvested, but the feast afterward. Good Friday only seems to be the finish. The death, the harvest we remember and we see before us taking place is not the end of the story. There is Easter event, a feast of victory. We look forward to Easter in hope because of a faith which is not based on our own accomplishments, no matter how good we believe we are. The faith we claim is based on something much more solid and firm . . . the Christ. The cycle of birth, life and death in which we ourselves are caught, as Christ was caught, has a different bottom line than we anticipated in our moments of distress.

I believe, as _____ did, as countless Christians before us, that because Christ lives, we too can live. By this uncommon hope we are joined together with love and trust. By this uncommon hope in the ultimate goodness of our God we are no longer afraid.

Amen

The Blessed Hope of Everlasting Life

Philippians 3:10-11

About the person: She was a life-long member of the parish, mid-fifties, with children and grandchildren in the congregation. Diagnosis had been sudden and death had come quickly to a vigorous woman. The sermon was given just prior to Pentecost and Confirmation.

When _____ was confirmed at Trinity church, a prayer was spoken for her and to her that we still retain in this season when we confirm other youth. The words said, *"the Father in heaven for Jesus' sake, renew and increase in you the gifts of the Holy Spirit, to your strengthening in faith, to your growth in grace, to your patience in suffering, and to the blessed hope of everlasting life."* . . . *renewing and increasing the gifts of the Holy Spirit:* When our Lord entered her life and claimed her as his own child in baptism, she was set to live among the people of God. In the midst of this company, she would learn about our Lord and his example of love. He would ask her repeatedly to become a channel of his love in all her life. She would share that love with a husband, shower it upon her children and find expression for it in a wider circle of our world. She learned of God's love and discovered a purpose in giving it beyond herself. We give thanks to our God that he daily renewed and increased the gifts of the Holy Spirit.

The Father in heaven for Jesus' sake, renew and increase in you the gifts of the Holy Spirit, to *your strengthening in faith* . . . God knows that often faith can grow weak. That's why he has so graciously given the church and the means of grace. Here we come to be strengthened, refreshed, nourished and nurtured. Here she came time after time for the occasion of hearing God's word and receiving his life-bestowing body and blood. She was one of those people who would always make eye contact with me as she came to the altar for communion. It was like an affirming glance saying . . . this is right, this is vital . . . this is for the strengthening in faith. God's word, his story, continues to draw me, to hold me. Worship matters!

The Father in Heaven for Jesus sake, renews and increases the gifts of the Holy Spirit, to our strengthening in faith . . . *to our growth in grace.* It dawns on us that life is a precious gift. We can't create it. We don't control it; we don't own it. Always, we are receiving it. Grace is God's free and unmerited forgiveness and love he brings to us. He is there for us even in times we don't think he is. During these long days of the hospital vigil, the family saw a little, anonymous story in the hospital you may have heard, but it tells the story. It says, "One night I dreamt I was walking along the beach with the Lord. Many scenes from my life flashed across the sky. In each scene I noticed footprints in the sand. Sometimes there were two sets of footprints, other times there was one only. This bothered me because I noted that during the low periods of my life, when I was suffering from anguish, sorrow or defeat, I could see only one set of footprints, so I said to the Lord, "You promised me, Lord, that if I followed you, you would walk with me always. But I have noticed that during the most trying periods of my life, there has been only one set of footprints in the sand. Why, when I have needed you most, have you not been there for me?" The Lord replied, "The times when you have seen only one set of footprints, my child, is when I carried you."

We grow in grace — the knowledge that the Lord picks us up, carefully cradles and holds. We grow in grace, to learn that life is not always from our perspective, our viewpoint, but even when we wrongly interpret it, God has been there *for us,* all the while.

The Father in heaven, for Jesus sake, renews and increases in us the gifts of the Holy Spirit, to our strengthening in faith, to our growth in grace *to our patience in suffering*. Suffering? Life is dotted with suffering until sometimes we think it's filled in the whole picture. It's unavoidable. No sidestepping the trouble. Not even our Lord. Suffering is so real in the cross: As real as an awful diagnosis, real in the hospital bed, real in the grave. Yet in the final days, _____ had patience in suffering. The prayer from her confirmation followed her: patience to fight the fight, patience to endure, patience finally to pass in peace.

The Father in heaven for Jesus' sake, renew and increase the gifts of the Holy Spirit, to our strengthening in faith, to our growth in grace, to our patience in suffering and *to the blessed hope of everlasting life. Everlasting life* is God's Good Word to us tonight here in this season of Easter. The Scriptures have sounded the trumpet call — the ringing, pealing, stirring, bell-banging of the New Testament faithful sounds out for us in no uncertain terms. Because he lives, we shall live. A Living Lord has come to make his home with us. He abides with us and we with him. Death is conquered by our Lord, and in His Resurrection, we see our hope! Why, "now the very vault of heaven can resound, in praise of love that still abounds, Christ has triumphed. Jesus is living. Alleluia!" _____ knew that. For us gathered here, we know that.

And we give thanks that we have seen a prayer come true for her as we pray it will for us! "The Father in heaven for Jesus sake, renew and increase in you the gifts of the Holy Spirit, to your strengthening in faith, to your growth in grace, to your patience in suffering, and to the blessed hope of everlasting life."

Amen.

Part 5. Funeral Preaching for Suicide Victims

A Conquered Enemy

1 Corinthians 15:26

This sermon was delivered at the funeral of a sixty-two-year-old man, the father of a large grown family. From all appearances of knowledge of his friends, he was in a comfortable financial situation with no real debt and a very satisfactory family circumstance. After a period of depression, he committed suicide.

The writer of the letter to the Hebrews says that "Here we have no lasting city, but we seek the city which is to come." Thus he points to the impermanence of our life, and emphasizes the hope of the Christian.

Sometimes, in periods when things are going fairly smoothly for us we succumb to the illusion, even though we know better, that the situations of life are quite permanent. Changes which we know must some day cease seem so remote as to be unreal. But we all know that at any moment something can happen to totally alter the pattern of life for us. In actual fact, nothing is permanent in this imperfect world. Life is always changing. Most of these changes we take more or less as a matter of course. We replace the furniture in our homes, change jobs, or even move from one place to another.

We think of most of these changes as advancements or improvements, and we rejoice in new opportunities. The growth and development and advancement of children, while sometimes regarded nostalgically, is generally viewed with satisfaction.

But many changes are not pleasant for us. The declining abilities of advancing age are often a burden to us, and a source of frustration. In the success oriented world of today the expectations that are placed upon us, and that we place upon ourselves, apply many subtle pressures upon all of us. Many of them bear their influence without us being aware of that influence, or without being able to control it. Sometimes they are more than we can cope with. But while the expectations of the world and of ourselves may be too demanding, the One who in tender love and sympathy said one day to those in need, "Let not your hearts be troubled . . . in my Father's house are many rooms . . . I go to prepare a place for you," is mindful of what we are able to bear and deals with us accordingly.

The one sure thing about life here is that it will end. And death always seems so final. So, no matter when or how it comes, death is the arch enemy of life. The loss of those we love, of immediate family members, sometimes without warning, probably requires our greatest adjustments in life.

Today we are faced with the loss of one who for many years has been a familiar member of his community; a family is faced with the loss of a husband and a father. When, in the midst of life and in comfortable circumstances, and with seemingly much to bring satisfaction to life, the unexplainables of life take from us one whom we loved and with whom we shared many satisfactions, we are suddenly brought face to face with that last great enemy of life which we call death. We realize then that with all our learning, with all our knowledge of health and disease, with all our understanding of the stresses and strains of life, and of our reaction to them, and with all the precautions we can take, we are sometimes helpless to delay the assault of that final enemy of life, which may come without regard to the portion of a normal life that has passed.

We have seen the sorrow and distress that death can bring as parents have had their hopes and dreams destroyed with the loss of a child, young people have been forced to grow to maturity without the love and guidance of a father or a mother, partner has been separated from partner, brother from brother, and friend from friend. Our efforts to withstand the attack of this enemy are sometimes bewilderingly ineffectual. Eventually, of course, death triumphs over all of us. Of all our enemies, this is the most victorious.

Yet, in spite of this, the victory cry of life can still be heard in the Christian gospel as it proclaims that even this enemy has been destroyed, and that one day that destruction will be complete. While death will be the last enemy to be destroyed, that destruction began, and was assured, with the resurrection of the Christ. In him almighty God has guaranteed us the victory. He was the "first-fruits" of those who are to be raised from the grave. As descendants of man, we are all to die. But in Christ we are guaranteed new life, free of all the separations and heartaches and bewilderments of our days here. The great Creator of man has provided not only this vale of tears for our experience and growth, but has ordained that beyond the grave the sun may break forth into a new and glorious day. Our Lord was victorious and is victorious in a battle that proved impossible for death to conquer. Now he lives and reigns; death has no more dominion over him, or over those who are his. His very purpose in coming was to bring life. We live in the joyous reality of this.

And we cannot be wrong in this, for the Holy Spirit himself confirms it to our spirits. This assurance has been part of man's experience for 2,000 years. Where death is the great destroyer, bringing one form of life to an end, Christ is the supreme life giver, the bread of life, the source of living water. He is the glorious sun of a bright new day.

Death, where it touches those we love, shatters our world. It brings heartache, distress, pain, and bewilderment; perhaps even a little bitterness and resentment as our stability is shaken. Death may be the last enemy to be destroyed, but in Christ the victory is ours in spite of circumstances. For the Christian, instead of it being the symbol of hopelessness and despair, death is but rest from labor and sorrow, release from pain, and an access into the very presence of God. In the face of death, with all its bitter pain and distress, we can still raise the triumphant cry, "Thanks be to God, who gives us the victory through our Lord Jesus Christ."

God's Love Is Deep

John 14:2-7

This sermon was delivered at the funeral of a young mother who committed suicide. It was written from the perspective of one who knows her as a pastor and friend.

The first time that I met _____ and _____ was seven years ago when I barged in on a birthday party at their home. This was the beginning of their relationship with our congregation, one that has deepened over these years. As we came to know and love _____ and _____ all the more, the more they selflessly gave of themselves. They both gave to the causes and concerns that they felt were important. _____ had a passion for wanting to have contemporary worship at Trinity, and was eager to give her opinions and be the mover of some great experiences. She spent many hours in Bible study — questioning and pondering the meaning of life and of her Lord. She experienced a renewal of life by the Holy Spirit, and continually reassured all of us that he is alive and present. She gave of herself to others willingly, even giving her eyes so someone else could see.

In one of our last lengthy conversations some weeks ago, we talked for a long time about the forgiveness of God and that nothing that we could ever do could separate us from him. She knew this in her heart, but as her illness increased and her highs and lows began to take its toll, we sensed that something was happening.

There was a war that was raging in her soul — her very being was being torn apart. The mind could grasp the meaning of what life is about, but there were times when it just didn't make sense any more.

Then the rising tide of despair must have rolled over her. Once again we are reminded of the complexities of the human soul (psyche). To some people we can easily make a separation between body and soul, but that is not Christian thinking, but rather Greek philosophy. The Greeks believed that the body and soul were joined together in life, and then as the body dies, the soul is released like a bird from a cage. The New Testament makes it clear that though there is both the flesh and the spirit, the two are bound up one with another. The New Testament uses the Greek terms, but the body and the spirit are linked together. We just don't save "souls", but we also are called upon to minister to the total person.

And because we are linked as a total being, when the innermost part of us is at ultimate war with the rest of us, something happens. The options of open doors seem to be closing one by one, there seems no other way out. The only way out that gradually overtook _____ and threw her over the cliff, took over her whole being, and an irrational act occurred. It was the only way to find the peace she yearned for so completely.

Jesus tells us that he can give the peace to his people that the world cannot give. We share his peace everytime here at Trinity we celebrate the Lord's Supper. This peace is more than the absence of pain and trauma: it is the very anesthesia of all of life. It is an entire different existence — beyond time and space. And as much as we humans love this world and will fight to save our lives, we will also long for a life free from the constraints of our human bodies.

There will be those today who will try to take God's task of judging _____. But we believe that we cannot do that. For in doing so, we are doubting the sufficiency of the grace and love of God. St. Paul, in the letter to the Romans, proclaims, "Who then can separate us from the love of Christ? Can trouble do it, or hardship, or persecution, or hunger or poverty or danger or death? No, in all these things we have complete victory; through him who loved us. For I am certain that nothing can separate us from his love; neither death nor life, neither angels nor other heavenly rulers or powers; neither the present nor the future; neither the world above nor the world below — there is nothing in all creation that will be able to separate us from the love of God, which is ours through Christ Jesus our Lord.''

We may doubt his power and love at times, but there is no doubt that he would have each and every one be his child. To be cradled in the loving arms of our heavenly father brings forth a yearning in the depths of the human soul. This is the peace _____ wanted to have so much. This is the rest from the war that waged within her — The Peace which passes all understanding has brought rest.

God's love is deeper than we can ever plumb and grasp. One day while a ship was in port a boy fell overboard — some sailors jumped into the water, pulled him out and tried to resuscitate him. The ship's doctor was not far off and they asked him if what they were doing was right. "Yes, you are doing all you can, and if you can't bring him around, you are doing all you can." A few minutes later the doctor experienced a twinge of conscience at his indifference and thought he would go and help. When he rolled the young man over, he saw it was his son. He was transformed in a moment. He began to use all he knew for his son's restoration, with the result that finally his son made a gasp for breath and lived. The surgeon helped him more than just because he was a doctor, but because his love for his child was awakened.

God isn't like that doctor, standing afar off when we jump into the murky waters of despair. Rather, God is continually standing near, ready to breathe into us his spirit and love. And just because, like rebellious children, we often do what is not pleasing to him, he still welcomes us with open arms. As prodigal children, he welcomes us home and shares the everlasting banquet.

We know that the Lord is loving _____ and will bring her to that life which has the joy and peace we all expect. Receive her, Lord, as your child and give her your peace that she couldn't find with us!

Part 6. Funeral Preaching for Cancer Victims

For a Cancer Victim   *Carl B. Rife*

Through the Valley of the Shadow

Psalm 23

This sermon was preached at the memorial service for an aunt who died of lung cancer.

Recently, while I was driving in Frederick, I had a rather lengthy wait at a stop light while a very long funeral procession went through the intersection. I must admit that my reaction was annoyance and impatience: I had things to do and places to go. But as I moved beyond my initial feelings I had a number of thoughts about the whole matter of death. My first thought was that every day in the city of Frederick and all over the world people die and there are similar processions that temporarily interrupt other people's journeys. Then I realized those funeral processions do not affect us too much unless we are part of the procession because of the death of someone we love. And then I reluctantly gave way to the thought that someday I will be the cause of someone else's temporary annoyance and impatience as they wait unknowing and uncaring for my funeral procession to clear the intersection.

What my musings point to is this: when someone we love dies, we become a part of the funeral procession and that entirely changes our perspective on the matter. Our concern then is not to get through the intersection as soon as possible. Rather our concerns lie at a different level. We feel the loss, the terrible emptiness left by the absence of one who occupied an important part of our lives. We seek assurance concerning the eternal destiny of the one we have loved. And we look at our own lives anew in the perspective of the hard core realities of life and death and the promises of God revealed to us in the written word of scripture and the living word in Christ.

Aunt _____ has passed through the Valley of Death. We feel her absence. We all will miss her. When the Christmas season comes and I am eating cookies I will especially feel the loss. Our tears are tears of loss. There is an empty spot in our lives because she is no longer with us.

Aunt _____ has passed through the Valley of Death. She was ready to face her Lord. Her faith rested in God's goodness and grace. And thus, with an assurance rooted in the God we know in Jesus Christ we can be comforted by the knowledge that she indeed is in God's loving care.

But the difficult thing is that Aunt _____ not only passed through the Valley of Death, for which we feel a loss and seek assurance, she also passed through the Valley of the Shadow of Death, marked by suffering, pain, and the fear of unknown aspects of death. The last few weeks were a difficult time for her. And it was difficult for her family and friends as they watched her struggle and suffer and could do so little to help. Those of us who visited her in the last days found ourselves at times breathing deeply, somehow hoping this would help her breathe.

Aunt _____ recent struggle and suffering dramatically reminds us that throughout our lives we all have walked, we all do walk, we all will walk at times through the Valley of the Shadow of Death. It is not death itself that causes us the most difficulty, it is the shadow cast by death throughout our life. From the moment of our birth we are caught up in the struggle between the forces of life and death, knowing that eventually the forces of death will have the last word. To state this is not to be morbid, but to face life realistically. Most of our life we spend ignoring or repressing this reality and that is another reason why the death of a loved one affects us so deeply, for we are brought face to face with the forces of death that lie within us.

Someone once summarized the entire history of the human race this way: they were born, they suffered, they died. There is a lot of truth in that. Life does have an uncanny resemblance to a soap opera which moves from one problem to another, interrupted only by brief periods of happiness and fulfillment, and not even the happiness and joy described in the Beatitudes.

But there is also reality and truth in the affirmation of the Psalmist who states that "Even though I walk through the Valley of the Shadow of Death, I will fear no evil, for Thou art with me". Amidst the hard realities of life and death is the promise of God that he will be with us. One of the creeds we use in our church puts it this way: "We are not alone. In life, in death, in life beyond death, God is with us. Thanks be to God."

Paul said it this way: "For I am absolutely certain that neither death, nor life, nor angels, nor principalities, nor things present, nor things to come, nor powers, nor height, nor depth, nor anything else in all creation, will be able to separate us from the love of God in Christ Jesus our Lord."

Christ himself repeated the promise: "Lo, I am with you always . . . " This is the promise that helps to ease our loss. This is the promise that gives us assurance about the eternal destiny of the one we have loved. This is the promise that helps us as we and our loved ones journey through the Valley of the Shadow of Death.

Beyond the Cross is the Resurrection. Beyond the Shadow of Death is the Light of the World. He who himself walked the Valley of the Shadow of Death on our behalf is with us. Through him we find life and light. Thanks be to God!

Not Defeated But Victorious

2 Timothy 4:7

Preached at a service of a boyhood friend who died at fifty after a long, painful struggle with cancer. His victory over his affliction was a great inspiration to family and friends.

In the Old Testament we read that one day King David was visibly shaken and sad of heart. A close friend, a loyal commander of his army, and a distinguished hero had been killed. When King David recovered from his shock he turned to his servants and said: "Do you know that a prince and a great man has fallen this day in Israel?"

As a servant of the King of kings, I say to you that a good friend of ours, a prince among men, and a humble person before his Creator has, in the love of God, left his earthly life for a new and glorious life in his Heavenly Father's home.

How appropriate it is that we who have known and loved _____ through the years can gather today in the sanctuary of his church to pay tribute not only to his days upon earth but to his faith in God as he knew Him through Jesus Christ.

I have known _____ all my life. We were boys together in Trinity Sunday church school. Through the years we have shared a warm, personal relationship of joys and sorrows, hopes and fears, and faith and doubts. If I were to take one verse from scripture to express his life and faith, perhaps no verse could be more fitting than the words of St. Paul: "I have fought the good fight; I have finished the course, I have kept the faith; henceforth, there is laid up for me a crown of righteousness."

Words are poor tools in this hour to express the thoughts which we feel within our hearts with the passing of our loved one and friend. The gap is always wide between our love and our words, our feelings and our speech. But in a simple way let us reflect upon a few of the blessings which this hour brings to our hearts and minds.

God has given to us two special gifts for moments like this. One gift is memory, that quality which enables us to look back over happy scenes and pleasant memories of yesterday. The other gift is hope, the vision to know that the shining sun is behind the heavy clouds of sorrow and loss which hang over us.

What a blessing a memory is! How thankful we are today that we can look back upon a few of the blessings which our loved one and friend has brought to our lives!

_____ life, like a diamond in the sunlight, sparkled with beauty and dignity at every angle. _____ felt a deep love and concern for all his friends. He was sensitive to their heartaches, their burdens, and their cares. How frequently he would ask about our problems; not to pry but in loving concern. When difficulties arose, regardless of what they were, you could always count on _____. He would never let you down or betray you. We are all thankful today for a loyal and true friend whom we cherish in tender memory.

His sense of humor was always evident even in his dying days. One noon during lunch he wanted to talk about this service which we now share. He said, "_____, don't make it sad. In fact, why don't you get some dancing girls for my friends to watch rather than have them listen to you." He was not being sacrilegious about death nor was he being rude to me. Humor, laughter and good fun were a part of his life. Humor is that God-given gift to keep our perspective straight when things become difficult. How necessary good humor is to our daily life.

_____ was a man of truth. Truthfulness for him was a basic way of life. As he saw it, truth involved more than just correct ideas and logic. It meant a spirit of honesty and loyalty in personal relations, a basic respect for every person, and the kind of conduct towards others which acknowledges the work of God in every human being. But I think especially this afternoon of the courage and cheerfulness which marked his life during his many long months of illness. Who of us could have walked in his footsteps with greater courage and more cheerfulness? We can only express the words of the disciple when he saw the victory of his Lord over the afflictions of life — "Thou art the man!"

How quickly and unexpectedly a threatening cloud can settle over us. Without rhyme or reason we find that our days are no longer carefree and gay. The hopes and dreams of our life suddenly vanish as we are confronted with problems and burdens which we never dreamed could be ours. How much we all have learned from _____ victory over affliction and his joyous spirit in spite of shattered hopes.

It has been said: "Faith grows a Christian, life proves a Christian, suffering confirms a Christian, and death crowns a Christian." Our loved one and friend who suffered so patiently, fought so valiantly, and loved so dearly has received a crown of life. His lingering illness was able to inflict suffering and pain upon his earthly body, but the illness could never touch his courageous spirit. While he was afflicted, he was not crushed. While he was perplexed, he was not driven to despair. While he was struck down, he was not defeated. Our dwelling place here is only temporary. We are not only the sons and daughters of men and women but we are also the children of God.

These are but a few of the joyous memories we treasure this day, memories which will help and encourage us when the light grows dim, when the pathway darkens, and when the day seems hopeless.

But God has also given us the gift of hope. _____ not only knew the meaning of life, but he knew the meaning of death. He knew the promises of Jesus when he said: "I go to prepare a place for you." "Where I am, there you will be also." He knew that to say "Goodbye" here, means to say "Good morning" in our eternal home.

During this past year _____ and I had lunch together on a number of occasions. One day last spring he asked me even before we had ordered our lunch: "Tell me all you can about death and life after death." We talked for nearly two hours. No punches were pulled. No questions were withheld. It was one of the frankest and most unemotional conversations about death I think I have ever had. When we left, he shook my hand and said: "Thanks for this noon. While I hope to beat it, I am not afraid to die. If I can't make it, I know that I will be with the Lord."

That is our hope. Death is not the end but the beginning. It is a sleep with a blessed awakening. It is falling asleep amidst the afflictions of life to awake amidst the joys of heaven. This is a victory celebration. We rejoice that in the mercy of God our loved one and friend has put aside his ailing body for a new and glorious spiritual body. We praise God that the pain of his earthly days has been exchanged for the glory of the eternal.

I want to share with you a story which I told him that day. One afternoon, a man, lying in a canoe close to shore, saw many beetles in the muddy bottom of the lake. He felt sorry for those lowly creatures which would never know any other world except gloom and mud and water. Then a big, black beetle came out of the water. He crawled up on the gunwale and sat there blinking at him. Under the heat of the sun the beetle died. Then a strange thing happened. His black shell cracked down the back. Out of it came a shapeless mass whose hideousness was transformed into a beautiful, brilliantly colored life. Out of that mass gradually unfolded four iridescent wings from which the sunlight flashed a thousand colors. The wings spread wide as if to worship the sun. The man realized that he had witnessed the transformation of a hideous beetle crawling in the mud to a gorgeous dragonfly soaring above the waters. The body that was left behind still clung to the gunwale of the canoe. While the dragonfly explored the wonders of his wings and his new world, the other beetles were still crawling in the mud. He knew that he had seen a miracle of nature. Out of the mud had come a beautiful new life. The thought occurred to him, if the Creator worked such wonders with the lowliest of creatures, what must be in store for his children created in his likeness!

That is our hope and our victory on this day. That is our comfort and our peace.

If _____ could speak to us this afternoon in his new joy, he might say with the poet:

I am home in heaven, dear ones;
Oh, so happy and so bright!
There is perfect joy and beauty

this everlasting light.
All the pain and grief is over,
Every restless tossing passed;
I am now at peace forever,
Safely home in heaven at last.

Did you wonder I so calmly
Trod the valley of the shade?
Oh, but Jesus' love illumined
Every dark and fearful glade.

And He came Himself to meet me
In that way so hard to tread;
And with Jesus' arm to lean on,
Could I have one doubt or dread?

Then you must not grieve so sorely,
For I love you dearly still;
Try to look beyond earth's shadows,
Pray to trust our Father's will.

There is work still waiting for you,
So you must not idly stand;
Do it now, while life remaineth —
You shall rest in Jesus' land.

When that work is all completed,
He will gently call you home;
Oh, the rapture of that meeting,
Oh, the joy to see you come!

Part 7. Funeral Preaching in Special Circumstances

Doing Battle With Death

Romans 8:14-39

The voice on the phone was _____ brother. He seemed able to say only a few words. _____ and _____ had found the baby in the crib suffocating. _____ held her while the life drained away. Then they had rushed out to the hospital.

It took a long time to get across the city and out to the far edge where _____ and _____ had moved, and I was too late. The nurse had a hard time telling me the baby was dead, and then she pointed out the door. "They've already gone." I ran out the door and down the ramp. Two figures, huddled back into their coats, were at the far end of the hospital making their way into the parking lot. I shouted, but there was no response. They just slowed their walk. I ran down the ramp. When I reached them, I was completely out of breath. It didn't matter. I had nothing to say.

For two days now all of us gathered here have been taking turns getting _____ and _____ attention. There have been tears and hugs and some awkward attempts at condolences. We have nothing to say.

We have gathered here today around this tiny casket hoping that by our presence we can say something that we cannot say with words. That's the first clue to coping with death — being present to one another. So it is that family and friends have gathered here today.

There is more presence here than the total of our concern. As we are present to one another, God is present here. The silence and grief of God are present here too.

You know the story, how God sent his only son into a cruel and purposeless world. The sign of the cross reminds us that God knows and understands the grief of a parent. This caring God who suffered the death of a child is here with us in our grief.

In our gathering there is a sense of impotence, of helplessness. We reach out to _____ and _____, but we also turn away in the agony of knowing there is nothing we can do or say to put things right again. Who can do battle with death?

Who indeed! Yes, it is a word to speak today! In the midst of our helplessness there is a parent God who comes to be with us and to share our grief, but this is also the God who has done battle with death and who has overcome it! Let the Church gathered here witness to the Good News that even this ultimate enemy, the enemy of death, has been vanquished by our Lord and Savior Jesus Christ!

Once there was a father who came to get help from Jesus because his little girl was sick. As he asked, the messenger came who said, "Don't bother. She is dead." It was to be a sign of the whole ministry of Jesus Christ that he went with that man, took the little girl by the hand, and said to her, "Talitha cum — Arise my child."

The real presence of this Christ is here with us today. He will understand and support us in our grief. He will also give us an assurance that death will not have the last word. While we are silent in the face of this death, Christ speaks. While we are helpless before this tragedy, Christ acts to assure us of eternal life. While we are afraid before the tombs of death, Christ comes forth as the Resurrection!

I remember that when _____ and _____ were married, some people said no good could come of it. There were people who said that the marriage of a black man and a white woman could only lead to tragedy. They seemed to be particularly afraid of a child of the marriage — a little child. It would be tragic, they said, if a child were born of a black man and a white woman.

They were afraid of little tragedies — of a few taunts, of some people's prejudice. Little did they know. The tragedy was not to be the life, but the death of the little child.

Now we are met here to get our perspectives straight. _____ and _____ and this child have helped us. Oh, how we need such children. Children to remind us we are all children of the one parent God. What a tragic loss it is to lose this child! We all mourn because we are coming to know how much we need the life of such a child.

Now we know. The silent grief of God demolishes the prejudices that thought the life of this child a tragedy. The death of such a child reveals the true tragedies of this world. The community that hesitated to celebrate the wedding now mourns together.

So God comes again. This gracious God embraces us. The Infinite grieves with us. This parent God lifts this little child from the fragile embrace of death and gives her new life in an eternal realm. In the death of this child, our eyes are opened. In the death of Jesus Christ, we are brought to newness of life. And so, people of God, gather around this miracle today. God has entered into our battle against the death of this child, and in this death we suddenly see the world in a new way. Be sure that the death we see here will not have the last word. Christ will bring this little child, too, to resurrection. Thanks be to God! Amen!

God Is Love

Psalms 121 and 23
Romans 8:31-39
Colossians 1:3-6 and 11, 12
1 John 4:7-21
Matthew 11:25-30
Mark 10:13-16
John 14:1-6 and 27

In our day the funeral of a child is an infrequent experience for a pastor. Nevertheless, each of us will encounter this situation without warning, and need to minister to it.

The background for this sermon was the death of a five and a half year old boy in a house fire. The dynamics which are recognized in dealing with the family include the presence of shock, guilt, and the ever-present question of why? First contacts with the family did not reveal all that they were feeling, and invariably, further contact and counseling will be needed. In this instance, the funeral service is an initial opportunity to open up some of the issues that may need to be addressed later.

In the scriptures we have read today, we have heard of the hope and trust that people express — hope and trust in God. It is very likely that these are not the feelings in our own hearts and minds these past several days. Nor can it be expected that any words today will easily bring such feelings to us.

We may, in fact, feel angry with God, left down by him. Or we may have feelings of having been assailed by the wrath of God, of being hurt and punished by him.

People of many times and places have experienced similar feelings in times of tragedy and sorrow. But those who have "waited on the Lord", meaning those who have patiently learned of God and looked for him in life, keep coming back to that which Jesus declared of him — God is love.

Our constant problem is to realize that for love to be genuine and real, it cannot be automatic nor can it be forced out of someone. If God had made us robots who could do nothing but love him, then he could also have insulated us from every harm and danger.

In a relationship in which we are free to love or not to love, however, we cannot be given the guarantee that nothing evil will ever happen to us. We clearly know that evil, in its attempt to pull us away from loving God, is often a very real fact of life. Evil is present in our own hardness of heart and in the pain and suffering which comes to us.

There is only one way to deal with evil — that is to seek God's help. Over and over again people have found that they cannot defeat evil on their own — but through the death and resurrection of Jesus Christ, God has shown us his power to win the victory over this enemy of us all. When we turn to God with trust and hope, evil is defeated and does not win us to bitterness and hatred and despair.

Though having him/her for only a short time, we can see in the childlike trust and love which _____ had the very qualities which we need to have in this hour and in the days ahead.

God gave up his only Son to die for us on the cross of Calvary. That is the all-the-way kind of love which shows us how very much God loves us. It is that kind of love that calls us to trust God.

First, we need to trust God to care for _____, now gone from us. We shall keep him in our memories, and know that God's love surrounds him still.

Second, we need to trust God to care for us, and to bring healing and comfort and peace to our troubled hearts. He can do this through his Word, and through persons of faith, and through the responses of our own lives to him.

Today we praise and thank God for the life of _____, and for what he/she has meant to us. We also submit our hearts to God, that he will keep us in his love until we walk with him face to face. Amen

Death on the School Playground   *Charles L. Koester*

For of Such is the Kingdom of Heaven

Matthew 19:12

_____ was ten years old when his life ended tragically through a childish experiment of holding his breath and attempting to render himself unconscious. I recall the trick was not uncommon when I was a child. Expelling all possible breath a fellow classmate was asked to hold you tightly in a bear hug from the back. On the school playground this was done to _____. Following release he staggered around, screamed, and fell to the ground unconscious.

It was later ascertained that oxygen did not reach the brain during the next minutes and _____ suffered ninety percent irreversible brain damage. Had he lived he would never have been the normal active fun-loving boy well known in church and school activities. He lingered unconscious for several days before he died.

In the usual sense there was no funeral. His body was immediately cremated. The family preferred a worship service at church on an evening. If a funeral can ever be a joy this service of worship was exactly that. God's spirit was there, and felt by all present. Over six hundred people were in attendance. Fellowship and support was offered to the family and to each other in a gathering following the service held in our parish hall.

The young man who held _____ during this experiment was also a member of the Church. We immediately counseled with him and his family and were *in constant touch with the school authorities. I spoke with the student body explaining that this was an accident and not the fault of anyone. Many students and classmates attended the service. The young man who held _____ we encouraged to serve as an acolyte. He did, and it helped in his healing of guilt.*

Prayer: Father, we pray for strength for this difficult time, for these difficult moments. Teach us acceptance of what we cannot understand. Teach us understanding of what we cannot change. Deliver us from the futile questioning and second guessing which come with our words, "if only." For our life, Father, is in your good hands. You give life, and sustain life, and grant eternal life. You, and you alone, know us individually in our depths. Keep us who sob our grief in the hand of your Son who saves us, and so holds _____ before your throne. We thank you, our Father, even through clouded eyes, that through your Son, another of your children, _____ so lives today in the eternity of your House. Amen.

We are here this evening as the People of God to express our joy. Yes, joy! Joy in spite of tragedy — Joy in spite of human ache and pain!

Joy, in spite of human loss of a loved one. Joy because, as the author of Hebrews expressed it, "This world is not our home; we look forward to our everlasting home in heaven." We are here to express that joy, that comfort, that support, to each other through the experience of worship. For this is not a funeral, but our joyful assurance of Christ's promise; "Because I live — you shall live also." And we comfort one another with his Words, even through our clouded eyes. We hear testimony in our worship this evening to our faith in the resurrection. Each of us now lives on this side of Easter. Because we do; we live in the realization that what we term death is not destruction, but deliverance.

And we are here this evening to learn a lesson from Jesus our

Savior and our brother. Our lesson concerns children. "Children," said Jesus, ". . . of such is the kingdom of heaven." Children — inheritors of eternal life. Children — befriended, understood, loved, blessed, by Jesus our Lord. _____, child of God — loved and understood by Jesus our Lord. _____, inheritor of eternal life lives in the Father's house. He lives in God's presence with more life than you and I who still remain in these mortal bodies. _____ lives with new life, new dimension, new understanding. For of such, children, promised our Lord, is the kingdom of Heaven. "Do not forbid their coming to me" he said. God our Father wants you who grieve to realize that! Jesus said it to us; "Do not forbid their coming to me." _____ is loved by the Father with an intensity that indescribably surpasses our human love for him. Jesus our brother says it; for he shakes us with the eternal reality of his words. Don't prevent your children from coming to me, even to coming to me where I now am. Don't try to keep them away from me though you humanly grieve. Because I'm here, Jesus says, I'm here on the other side in life after life. Let even the children come to me, don't prevent them, for of such (children) is the Kingdom of Heaven. That is the lesson of worship this evening. _____ has new life, loved, understood, understanding, a total joy which we who still remain in this body will never experience until we are where _____ is, in the Father's House. And even in our tears, our unanswerable questions we humanly ask, the explanations we humanly demand . . . Even here is the positive loving proclamation of God's Son — Don't try to keep this child back with you. Don't try to keep him back through your futile questions. Don't try to keep him back with you through those personalized "if onlys." Christ has promised us, "_____ is with me."

Children ask me occasionally what death and going to heaven is like. I explain it in this way by saying; Remember when your parents had a party or a get together at your house? Perhaps the closet wasn't large enough to hang up all the coats of the people who came, so they laid them all on your bed. And when your bedtime came, your parents said to you. It's just too much work to move all those coats, so you go sleep in our bed in our bedroom. And after our guests leave and they take their coats, we will put you back in your own bed. And so they did. You went to sleep in Mom and Dad's bedroom, but you woke up in your own. So it has been for _____, so it will be for each of us. We go to sleep in this world, but we wake up in the Father's house. In this is our joy as God's people! Yes, joy! Joy because there is a homecoming because there is a home. _____ so lives in the Father's house, and in worship tonight we acknowledge our Father's love and kindness. And even through human grief and tears we would still proclaim in our worship. Thank you, Father. Thank you so very much. But for us, God has called us not to eternal life as yet. He has called us to live in this present. In our frail humanness our separation from a loved child appears tragic. For _____; joyous, for us human loss. Humanly we do not see things from God's viewpoint and perspective. Even here God says, "Look, it is not yours to know as yet my eternal plans and motives in the scheme of things." Ours is to trust the Father who proves his love for each of us by sending his Son to die for us that each of our deaths is not eternal. Ours is to trust God's Christ and our savior who says;

> *I am with you always,*
> *I love you.*
> *Cast your burdens on me because I care for you.*
> *You will never die,*
> *You will have eternal life.*

Ours is to trust, to trust the promises of our Savior and our brother in human suffering and pain and sorrow. God may not answer our questions, but he does fill our question marks with his presence, his living presence. We may not see the "whys" but one day we will as St. Paul said, "Be face to face."

And to you people of God at worship tonight who are relatives, friends, neighbors. May God lead you to help and comfort this family in acts of love and kindness and understanding. For God has called you to be instruments of his love. And may we all be found in Christ Jesus who redeems our grief by emptying himself that we might be full. And in that fulness, find even in these moments; Joy In The Lord!

Kim's Wish Come True

John 14:2

I will begin my sermon today talking about a horse. More specifically my focus will be a horse's name. The horse of which I speak is the one owned by Kim. I speak of that horse, not because Kim loved horses, although she did. I speak of that horse, not because Kim was an athlete, although she certainly was. I speak of Kim's horse because of the horse's name. Kim named him, "Kim's Wish Come True".

Kim must have named her horse with this unusual name because, in fact, the horse was a wish come true for her. Of course, I will not speak about the horse, but the fulfillment of Kim's wishes and a number of connections between this name and Kim's Christian life.

It was Kim's wish come true to be baptized. She was baptized on Sunday, October 30, 1977. She died just two weeks later on Sunday, November 13, 1977. Some months prior to her being baptized she had indicated her desire to be baptized, confess her faith in Jesus Christ as Lord and Saviour, and thus become a part of God's family, the Church. For about two months she attended a class of instruction. It was not always easy for her to attend, because of her physical condition. Nevertheless, she attended the sessions and indicated that she had learned a great deal from them.

On Sunday, October 30th, she had to arise at 3:00 a.m. so by the time she came to church she would be stable. Kim was frequently dizzy, especially when she first got up in the morning. To assure the fact that she would be able to participate in the 8:00 a.m. worship service, she arose at 3:00 a.m. When Kim wanted something, she was willing to make the appropriate sacrifices to get it. She wanted to be baptized.

She told me just a few short weeks ago that it was her desire to be baptized originally, because she was afraid that she would be punished for not being baptized. She also indicated that she had come to a much more positive and holistic view of Baptism through the classes. She wanted to be baptized because she knew God wanted her as a part of his family.

We had considered the possibility of Kim being received at an evening service because of her physical condition. We spoke of the possibility of November 6th at the evening service. If we had waited until Sunday, November 6th there would have been serious difficulty, because Kim had to go to Rochester, Minnesota to Mayo's Clinic that day. It was good timing that Kim was received into the Church by Baptism on October 30th. She also received her first Communion that day. It was for her a wish come true.

Another wish for Kim was to be with her Heavenly Father. While she did not expect to die as early as she did, she knew that death must be faced by all. Eternal life is not something that is earned, but is a gift from God for those who believe in him and accept him as their Lord and Saviour. Kim came to an understanding that she could be with the Father through faith in Christ. She came to understand that God intersects our lives, becomes a part of our lives before we die, as well as bringing us to his Kingdom in fulfillment of his promise after we die.

Kim knew that through faith in Jesus Christ she would be with the Father in Heaven when she died. She came to understand that heaven is not given as a reward for those who have done good deeds, but a gift which comes to sinners from a gracious and merciful Father.

Kim's wish to be with the Heavenly Father came true. From our time schedules it came too soon. Our time schedules do not always determine what will happen.

In addition, Kim had another wish. That wish was that her family and friends would be with her. Just before she went into surgery at Mayo's Clinic she said, "I'll see you all later." She was, of course, thinking of seeing her family after surgery. The words, however, have wider implications in that Kim never fully recovered from that surgery. Since coming into the church by Baptism, she indicated her feelings that she would like her friends and family to become a part of the Christian faith. New Christians are like that. They want to share what they have found with others. We therefore consider Kim's words in the larger context, namely that Kim would like to see us all later before the throne of God. It would be for her a wish come true: "I'll see you all later," she said.

One of the rooms which God surely has reserved for those who believe in him will be marked, "Reunion Banquet . . . Kim, Hostess."

A Hand We Can Grasp

John 14:1-6

This was a Funeral Sermon for two young people who disappeared from the community and whose remains were found many weeks later.

As a parent of two young men, ages eighteen and twenty, I've tried this past week to put myself in the place of _____ and _____'s parents and their families. But I cannot. All I can do is to do what each one of us can do — to go with them into the depths of their sorrow and despair and walk with them along the road of this tragic chapter in their lives.

One of the things that I wonder each time my sons leave home is will they come back safely? Youth are like that — they like to go and to do. We as parents can't keep them locked up in our homes. We must let them have their freedom so they will learn to make their choices and decisions. This they must do in order to become responsible adults.

_____ and _____ were like that, too — they loved to go to tractor pulls, to fairs, to the Fort Fest. As much as we like, we would do anything to turn the clock back and say, "If only they had not gone to that wedding reception on that fateful night." Or, "We should have been with them."

If only we could go with them to protect, to help, to assist them in making the decisions that are in their best interest. But we can't. They must leave their father and mother — they must go out on their own.

So as our children and youth leave our homes, they only have the Lord to be with them and if, in the early years, their religious education and the example set by us as parents — to follow in faith — we know that they do not go out alone. The Holy Spirit is with them, our Lord in his marvelous ways walks before them. He is with them no matter where they go, no matter what they do. They are never alone. This is Jesus' promise in our gospel lesson, which we read tonight. "I go to prepare a place for you." What a comfort to know. Like ourselves, the disciples were confused. They had walked with Jesus for three years, they had depended upon him, they felt safe with him. But now he tells them that he must leave. "But I go to prepare a place for you."

As children of the Heavenly Father, it is good that we have his hand to grasp as we follow his leading — through the darkness of death. We know that as individuals each one of us must die alone — even if we are in the midst of a family or with friends. But spiritually speaking, we never die alone. Just like in life, we are also never alone — we can always reach out to the strong hand of the Lord and place our feeble, frail hand in his.

There once was a little boy who had wanted desperately to see the factory where his father had worked for many years. But the company policy stated that no children could be in the plant while the machines were working. So one night the father took the lad to the place, but it was totally dark. The boy looked around at all of the myriad of machines and the labyrinth walkways that weaved in and about the huge building. Quickly he took his father's strong, calloused hand and said, "You go first, Dad, you have been here before in the daylight." So the father and son walked safely in the dark to the place where each day the dad came to his station in the middle of the factory. The father had been there in the day, so he knew how to find his way in the dark.

In this darkness of death, we, too, have a Father whose hand we can grasp. And we know that he will safely lead us through the darkness into the light once again. He leads us to a place where we join with him — in the glory of his presence. To be with the Lord is really what every Christian desires. And because Jesus traveled the Hell of the Cross and the wait in his grave, this is only a temporary thing — for his promise is to take away the darkness — to open once again the eyes of _____ and _____, that they might blink in the heavenly light once more.

To live eternally in the lightened presence of our Creator is the goal of each and every believer. This promise gives us comfort, hope and strength. To return to our real home — the place where the Lord has prepared for those who have faith and walk that path in life.

The vision of that place is far more glorious than we can ever imagine. The words of Revelation, Chapter 21:1-4, give us a clue. "Then I saw a new heaven and a new earth; for the first heaven and the first earth had passed away, and the sea was no more. And I saw the holy city, new Jerusalem, coming out of heaven from God, prepared as a bride adorned for her husband; and I heard a great voice from the throne saying, 'Behold, the dwelling of God is with men. He will dwell with them and they shall be his people and God himself will be with them; He will wipe away every tear from their eyes, and death shall be no more, neither shall there be mourning nor crying nor pain anymore, for the former things have passed away.' "

_____ and _____ are rejoicing in their home. They have safely made their journey. Let us renew our faith — so that like them, we walk in the light of our Lord. To that place he has prepared — where there is no more mourning, crying or pain. May this help us to wipe away our tears tonight.

Redeeming Grief

1 Corinthians 15:55-57

A young couple, married for about a year, joined our parish. When they purchased a new home some distance away, they faithfully drove the distance to worship each Sunday. One could see a deepening and growing commitment they possessed for the church.

On the eve of New Year's they purchased a new car. New Year's day brought the beginnings of a blizzard. About noon they went out to pick up a newspaper and decided to enjoy a short drive in spite of the weather. On a slippery road the car began to skid, hit a rut, spun sideways and crashed into an oncoming car. She was killed instantly. He, a Vietnam veteran, sustained multiple fractures of the leg which hospitalized him for the next six months. His recovery was long and filled with many medical complications. He almost died at one point during surgery.

At the funeral all were in tragic shock. The young husband was filled with guilt over the accident and his being unable to be present at his wife's funeral. For him the whole tragedy was most unreal. And when he would return home, six months later, it would still be unreal.

Immediately following the funeral we visited him with a copy of the sermon. We read and discussed. Visits in the hospital were frequent and he was able to be open with his feelings and able to communicate. His Christian faith and his battle not to withdraw held him in good stead. Today, he is back in church life making healthy adjustments. He has been bringing a girl friend to church. Life is going on. Two years after the accident, they were making plans to be married.

Prayer: Father, we pray for strength for this difficult time. For these difficult moments. Teach us acceptance of what we cannot understand. Teach us understanding of what we cannot change. Deliver us from the futile questioning and second guessing which come with our words, "if only." For our life, Father, is in your good hands. You give life, and sustain life, and grant eternal life. You, and you alone, know us individually in our depths. Keep us who sob our grief in the hand of your Son who saves us, and so holds _____ before your throne. We thank you, our Father, even through clouded eyes, that through your Son, another of your children, _____, so lives today in the eternity of your House. Amen

In these terrible moments of tragedy that engulf a young husband unable to be here, in these moments that engulf family, relatives, neighbors, and friends who are here this morning, several questions loom large before us. We have each asked these questions ourselves. We have asked them together. Why _____? Why so young? Why this way? Why? "If only a car ride were not taken." "If only the roads were not icy." "If only the rut were not there." "If only the car had not skidded." We each ask those kinds of questions with our "whys" and "if onlys."

The answers to those ultimate questions we do not possess, nor can any fellow human being give them to us. From our human reason, we attempt to reach logical and rational conclusions, but to this tragedy of life's termination, logic and reason do not apply. We know this. We know this with a certainty. Yet, we still insist, in our own and individual and several ways, on being logical.

We will not so find an answer to those questions we ask from our depths. Yet we cannot dismiss our questioning, try as we will.

Our questions are human, and we are human.

Questions, questions, all kinds of questions. Also present are our resentments, and those feelings of being cheated. Even God takes his share of our questioning abuse. And we hurt. We hurt very much. Our grief in this tragedy is deep from inside us where we really live. Our feelings and our emotions are part of our humanness.

You each sit here, as I stand here, with your own set of questions. Questions, which to be brutally honest, for which none of us will find the answers.

However, we have an alternative to our questioning, our grief, our feelings of injustice and anger. It is God's alternative, and I would bring it to each of us here this morning. As you are able in these moments, please listen as you can.

We can live life now, and from this day forward, in a futile, endless, bitter grief, a grief which questions, but will find no answers. St. Paul put it pointedly, as he said, "Truly, if our hope in Christ were limited to this life only, we should, of all men, be most miserable." The other alternative: we can live life now, and from this day forward, in a redeeming grief. A grief that will again see the light of day, as it sees, as well, the light of eternal life.

Even in sorrow we do have hope, and eternal hope is so clearly ours in Jesus Christ. That is what Christmas, Good Friday, and Easter are all about. He was born, he lived, he died, he rose, alive again! His empty tomb proclaimed that we are not empty. His ever living presence within us can fill us with the very presence of God.

_____ is with God her Father, through Christ, the one whom she claimed as her Savior. She has more life today than any of us who are here. The certainty of our faith tells us this, strengthens us, comforts us, and yes, redeems our grief.

"He who believes in me shall never die, but shall have everlasting life," said Christ. This assurance of our Lord is the beginning of our redeeming grief. We know where _____ is, and who she is with. Jesus Christ assures us, "_____ is with me. She is with me in my Father's House." With this assurance, our grief is redeemed, and we can continue to face life in this world with steady eyes. For even in this tragedy, there is the strength, and assurance of life's destiny. Because of Jesus, God's Son, we are more than our bodies.

To you who loved _____, in your grief, and loss, behind it all, underneath it all, in those empty places where you really live, Christ is present and ready to fill you with himself and with the presence of God. In loneliness, heartache, frustration, he says, "Cast your burdens upon me, for I care for you." God's Christ can redeem your grief, and give you God's peace that passes even our human understanding of it.

Death, even _____'s death, is swallowed up in victory through Jesus Christ. _____ lives! What a great comfort and strength it is to lean on the strong assurance of our Lord who said, "Because I live, you shall live also."

Life without such certain assurance of destiny would be a cruel joke played by a capricious God. A God whom all of us would reject. But God does not laugh from his Heaven at the hell of our heartache. He does not turn away from us, as we are so prone to turn away from him. Nor is he silent during the long night of our anguish of soul at the time of tragedy in the loss of a wife, a daughter, a friend. Nor does God leave us as empty, hollow shells of misery in our grief. No. God will have none of that!

Listen to the words of the Psalmist:

> *The Lord will give strength unto his people.*
> *The Lord will bless his people with peace.*

You are the people of God. His people. And he will fill you with his peace and presence. Thanks be to God for the victory, even over death, through Jesus Christ our Lord.

God's people, in these difficult times and moments let us comfort one another with the hope, strength, and assurance of God's Word. Allow God's sent Son to redeem your grief. _____ is in God's good hands, in God's good House. Because Christ's victory is eternal, our separation from a loved one is not eternal but temporary. Let us comfort one another with the victory Christ has accomplished for our lives, and for our faith.

_____ has abundant life eternal. And even in our tears, we would say, "Thank you, God. Thank you very, very much."

Victory Over Evil

Romans 8:31-39

This meditation was given at the funeral service of a thirty-seven-year-old woman who was shot by her estranged husband and before her death, lay in the intensive care unit of the hospital for nearly seven months — most of the time in a coma.

It is good to see this large crowd here. It shows your support for the family of _____. Yet most of you, even as you reach out in support, are echoing the question of St. Paul in some form. Paul had great insight and sensitivity. He poses the question for us, "What then shall we say to this?" And we are asking with Paul: Why? What then shall we say?

Certainly none of us has all the answers. But of some things we can be sure. During the last seven months we have participated in and been witness to two things: the power of sin and evil and the triumph of love.

We are here today to worship and to receive the assurance from God Almighty of support and comfort. We hear the good news of the resurrection to eternal life. "I am the way and the truth and the life." "Death is swallowed up in victory."

But we come here also with a variety of emotions because of the nature of this death.

Relief that a long ordeal is over for _____, her family and friends.

Anger that this death was such a waste of life.

Fear that forces are loose among us that can cause such havoc and pain.

Remorse for not being more supportive of the family.

Sorrow, even *bitterness,* over the loss of a life in her prime and for one who could do such a thing.

And yes, some feelings of *forgiveness*.

And for all of us *hope*.

"What then shall we say to this?" The burning question of why? I don't know why completely. There is no clear answer to many questions in life and death. Job wrestled over the question of the suffering of an innocent man.

And though I don't know why completely — I still see through a glass darkly — I do have some insights from the Word of God. This death is not God's will. It is tied in with the forces of evil. That struggle goes on all the time. Wars take the lives of thousands, even millions. Hatred and jealousy and fear destroy. Death is tied closely with evil. It is the final enemy.

I said we have been part of two things, the power of sin and evil and the triumph of love. We are not alone. We have hope. We have a Savior. He who did not spare his own son comes to us with understanding, compassion, forgiveness, and love. Yes, the power of love has been present these last seven months. It has been present especially in you who have reached out to touch the family.

_____ had a very critical night about three weeks after her hospitalization. The family was called in. My wife and I and several others spent the night with them. At one point we went into her room early in the morning. We witnessed a beautiful sunrise through the window, dawn in the East. It reminded me of the words of Isaiah 58:8. "Then shall your light break forth like the dawn." It was like the rainbow after the flood. The Lord Almighty continues to be supportive.

I can't answer all your questions or mine. When you leave this service you will still have some emotions of which you are not sure. But of some things we can be certain. God loves us. He wants the best for us. In the midst of sadness let us learn to be grateful for the happy experiences, the good memories. _____'s son showed wonderful insight when he said to his grandmother, "We must not be bitter." Bitterness destroys and blocks the good memories.

The Lord God comforts and supports. He holds out to us the hope of the resurrection and eternal life. John Greenleaf Whittier, the Quaker poet shares with us ". . . and love can never lose its own." What a beautiful insight to help lessen grief. Whittier surely based this truth on Romans 8, "Who can separate us from the love of Christ?"

Jesus shows us the way ahead. We have a glimpse of heaven, "In my Father's house are many rooms." It caused Paul to shout out, "Thanks be to God who gives us the victory."

Underneath are the everlasting arms. We may leave here with some unanswered questions. But we leave with the peace of God that passes all understanding. "In all these things we are more than conquerors through him who loved us." Love has triumphed over evil. Alleluia!

Amen

Where To Go When You Grieve

Matthew 14:12

This funeral sermon was preached for a forty-year-old member of my congregation; he died after an illness of six weeks, leaving a wife and two teenage daughters.

What do you do and where do you go when a loved one dies? Where do you go when you have a pain in your heart that no physician can cure? Where do you go when you feel like you've swallowed a stone? Where do you go when the heaviness of your grief is like a staggering load? Where do you go when tears run down like rain on your face? Who will care enough? Who can help? Who will understand, *really* understand your grief?

There is an old gospel song which asks the same question:

Life here is grand with friends I love so dear,
Comfort I get from God's own Word;
Yet when I face the chilling hand of death,
Where could I go but to the Lord?

Our text today comes out of a fresh grief and a terrible loss caused by death too. John the Baptizer has vigorously denounced Herod and his adulterous relationship with his brother Philip's wife. Herodias is enraged and when Herod's birthday is celebrated she cunningly contrives the death of John the Baptizer, that dauntless preacher who has named her sin. The final result is that John is beheaded. The grieving disciples of John come and claim his body, give it a loving burial, and then "went and told Jesus."

That is where we are today. Your dear, loved one has died, you are now giving the body the service and burial that befits one so precious to you, and then — then, what do you do, where do you turn, where do you go with a nearly unbearable pain and unanswerable questions? The text gives great comfort and counsel in this hour: they "went and told Jesus." Why don't we try that? Why don't we go to Jesus too? Let's go to Jesus!

Why?

Go To Jesus Because He Cares

John's disciples knew it would make a difference to Christ, that it would matter to him that their friend and leader and loved one had died — and it *still* matters to him. He still cares when we hurt. Do you recall the plaintive question in the familiar song?

Does Jesus care when I've said good-bye
To the dearest on earth to me,
And my sad heart aches, till it nearly breaks —
Is it aught to Him? does He see?

And the glad response is:

0 yes, He cares — I know He cares!
His heart is touched with my grief;
When the days are weary, the long nights dreary,
I know my Savior cares!

"I *don't* care" is one of the most hurtful phrases we can hear when we are in pain. But those who *do* care; family, friends (those who have called at your home these past days, those who have brought food, those who have called with sympathetic messages, those who have sent flowers, those who are at this service today, those who will continue to support you and help you) — all of this is immeasurable help in your need. But think of the added glory and wonder of this: Jesus, the Divine Son of God, cares too! He is more touched with your grief than anyone. That's why we go to him: he cares!

Go To Jesus Because He Loves Our Dead

John's disciples knew that Jesus loved him too. Had Jesus not said, "Among men born of women, there is not a greater than he?" And so *your* loved one — this husband and father and friend of so many of us — was loved by Jesus too. Jesus had claimed him as his very own son when in repentance, faith, and baptism he became his own possession. Jesus walked with him through the illness, and also "through the valley of the shadow of death", and then into heaven's bright home. Jesus has never forsaken him, and now he welcomes him, rewards him, keeps him — keeps him safe for you until the day of reunion.

We need never fear for those loved ones of ours who fall into death. In Christ's death and resurrection he has taken the sting away from our dying, and promises us only peace and light.

A man walked a lonely, difficult, treacherous mountain-pass late one night. He knew if he made one misstep he would tumble to certain death on the rocks hundreds of feet below. Nearing the top, his foot slipped off the narrow path and he fell. He scrambled and grabbed finally, on his descent down, a small bush, and barely caught hold of it. He cried for help, he prayed, he called, he tried to get a tighter grip, knowing all the while that his strength was leaving and he would surely fall. Finally he lost his strength, and fell — fell just six inches to solid ground beneath his feet!

So with our loved ones: they fall — they fall into the hands of death, fall into the great Unknown, falling, falling, falling, and fall into the everlasting and loving arms of a Father God who holds them secure. No wonder we sing in relief, "Safe in the arms of Jesus, safe on His gentle breast."

Go To Jesus Because He Will Help Us

The disciples of John knew Jesus not only loved him, but also would help them.

So you — Jesus wants to help you, too. He helps us by reminding us of his victory over death that means our loved ones are safe — but brighter days are ahead for us too. Your grief is almost despair today, but this is not the end. There is more, there is strength, there is promise, there is reunion, there is hope!

A husband and wife had been missionaries in Korea for fifteen years. They had worked side by side in the Gospel of Christ. And now she is dying. The broken-hearted husband held her hand until her departure. But just before she died she said, "Do not grieve for me, my dear. You'll get me back again, you'll get me back." A month later their only child died of the same disease as his mother. The man's heart was crushed; he'd lost his wife, and now his son. But as the boy died he said, "Don't cry. I see a light. I see mother. I see Jesus. And remember, Dad, you'll get us back again." The father sat in a funeral train, taking his son to be buried by his mother. Two Korean women sat behind him. One was weeping. Her companion asked her why she was crying and she replied, "O, I feel so sorry for the missionary — he lost his wife and son in such a short time." The other woman said, "Don't cry for him — Weep for yourself and for me. I lost a boy and may never get him back. You lost a daughter and may never see her again. But these Christians who know Jesus have a strange way of getting back their dead!"

And we do! We see our loved ones again. One of the best things I can tell you is that "Christians never see each other for the last time!"

What Shall I Do? Where Shall I Go?

The text today, then, tells us where to go with our grief: you "go and tell Jesus." There is a painting which shows the devil at a chessboard with a young man. The devil has just made his move and the young man's face has the look of one whose king is check-mated. On his face is written defeat and despair. One day, Paul Morphy, the great chess genius, stood looking at that painting. Carefully he studied the positions on the board. Suddenly his face lighted up and he shouted to the young man in the painting, "You still have a move — don't give up, you still have a move!" So today, you weep, you hurt, you despair, you think you are in a corner, all your next moves are blocked. Oh, no, they aren't! Go to Jesus! He is your Friend, he loves you, and he will help you!

Death of a Down's Syndrome Adult　　　　　*W. George Easson*

The Room Named Heaven

John 14:2, 3

This sermon was used at the funeral of a thirty-seven-year-old afflicted with Down's Syndrome. He never acquired the ability to speak even a few words. He was kept at home and cared for throughout his life by his parents. He died after only a very short illness.

What is it that gives value to life? In the eyes of the world it is intelligence and the ability to produce. Great importance is placed upon the Einsteins, the Salks, the Menningers, the Shakespeares and the Lincolns of the world whose brilliance and ability have shaped human society and produced the tide of technical and intellectual advances which almost overwhelm us today. Those with leadership qualities who are able to influence others; those with persuasive or political or intellectual or athletic power who can inspire others, gain approval, and create excitement are the people of worth. Those are the lives the world values.

On that basis, most people have some value. But it happens at times that there are those who are denied the normal capacities the rest of us take for granted; those who require unusual amounts of care and attention. For those with the responsibility of providing that care, it does not take long to discover that there are other human qualities of much greater significance in determining the value of life. They soon learn to value life by other things than productive capacity. Things like love and trust, sympathy and patience, honesty and a transparent spirit are infinitely greater indicators of real value to life.

These things have the ability, even in very uncomplicated situations, to create strong relational bonds, which, in the final analysis, are what declare life to be of value. Two things in particular deepen and strengthen relationships. One is need and dependency. It is the helplessness of an infant in the first few months of life that stirs the initial wells of love in a parent.

The other bonding factor is sacrificial service and devotion. As the dependent individual feels the security that devotion provides, the depths of love are plumbed in him or her. There are many difficulties associated with this kind of relationship. Over a long period of time it is physically very difficult to bear the responsibility of meeting the needs of someone who is highly dependent, yet in spite of problems and limitations, there exists something creative in the relationship and the bonds that are forged are strong.

But then when the responsibility is over and the labor of love is ended there is an urgent need to hear again the assurances of our faith. We need to hear again the affirmation which gives confidence that the one who is gone from us is now in a more creative and fulfilling situation than we could provide; that he is in the care of hands more omnipotent than the ones which have served until now, and that he is under the shadow of a love even more appealing. For this, we have the comfort and the glory of the faithfulness of our Lord.

"In my Father's house are many rooms," Jesus said. "I go to prepare a place for you." Up to the time of Christ, all people thought there were two worlds — one of earth and sky and sea, of clasping hands and loving hearts; and another world into which all passed at death; a chill and cheerless, lifeless place, which at best, was robbed of all that made for pleasantness; a place where life was nothing more than dazed existence.

But when Christ came he declared that there was but one world, all under the direction of the one God. Heaven is his throne; earth is his footstool. All the universe of created things is God's house. Earth with its green fields, its majestic mountains, its steadfast hills, is one room. Heaven, which outshines the earth in infinite ways, is another room. There is a life to be lived with the Father here, but there is a limitless and expanding life of glory and peace and boundless fulfilment to be lived with him there.

"I am going to prepare a place for you . . . And after I go and prepare a place for you, I will come back and take you to myself."

Life is characterized by movement out into the world. Children move out into the world to get an education and to begin to take their place in the social life of the community. Later they go out to join the work force and to provide for their own needs. Often young children will go out to help work on some club project or to visit or play with a friend. Then, when evening comes, their father will go out to where they are with the word that it is time to come home, and he will take them home with him. There may be a reluctance to leave what they are doing, but there is something about going home that is appealing and that feels very right. It is the proper place to be.

For each of us, the time comes when at the end of the day a kindly, interested and concerned Father comes to us and interrupts the activity of the day with the word that it is time to come home, then he gathers us up securely and takes us home with him. He takes us home! There may be some reluctance to leave what we are doing, but it is the proper place to be. That is where we find security. That is where everything is regulated to serve our best interests. That is where love enfolds us with a peace which washes away the strains, the hurts, and the anxieties of the day. That is where we know we belong. That is where we can grow and rest in comfort in the presence and under the protection and care of a love that cannot wish anything but good for us.

"I will come back and take you home." He has now come to yet another of us with the word, "Come, it is time to go home." As he takes him, we who are left rejoice in the comfort of the promise that those who walk with God go back home to the peaceful security and joyful presence of the Father's love where learning is forever expanding, and where relationships are perfected and all life is glorified. Oh the depth of the joy and the security and the comfort of the Father's promises and of his love.

Part 8. Funeral Preaching for Those
Without Church Membership

The Journey of Life

Psalm 122
Luke 24:13-35

In many communities across our country, Pastors, like myself, are called upon frequently to preside over funerals for a person who had no affiliation with the local congregation. In many instances the family did not have a congregational affiliation either. This sermon has been effective in many such situations.

I think of life as being like a journey. We travel through each day of life as though it were a trip. We hope, we plan, we look forward to what is ahead. We enjoy the present and remember the good times of the past. As we travel the road of life, we encounter some surprises along the way. We find unexpected hardships, delays, and problems.

Today, we pause for a moment having encountered an unexpected delay. We pause for a moment in our journey of life to celebrate and remember our sister, wife, mother, friend. We pause to give thanks to God for having been able to walk the road of life with her, for having the privilege of knowing her, and of sharing life with her. Today we come together with our own memories of that life shared. We come with our own stories of travels, encounters, and remembrances. We come to share those memories and experiences. We come to remember that each was a gift from God, given as a blessing as we have walked along our journey of life.

We also pause in our journey to be refreshed and renewed in order that we can travel on. We pause to renew and restore our hope and our confidence in a kind, loving God. We pause to share our faith so that as we move on to the future, we might be able to recall the past and enjoy the gifts of the present.

To find hope and confidence, we turn to the Scriptures which are the witness of faith of persons who lived long ago. They are the faith statements of persons who also traveled along the road of life and found it necessary to pause for some time to renew their faith and regain their trust in God. In both cases, we hear the words of persons who suffered distress, discouragement, pain, and alienation. They were persons questioning their lives of faith. They were seeking hope in the middle of what seemed to be hopelessness. They wanted peace in their distress.

The Psalmist speaks of his life as being like a trip. In the trip, he imagined he found hope from the very beginning, from the very first time he was invited to travel. From the first stages of planning, there was hope. But this trip was unlike any other trip. It was the trip home — the trip to the new Jerusalem, the center of all hope and faith. The temple was in Jerusalem, the center of all things, a place of security. The people believed God was present in the temple. The temple was the center of worship. It was there in Jerusalem, and only there, that the faithful could feel the presence of God. It was only in Jerusalem that God and all His presence, comfort, peace, fairness, and salvation could be felt, recognized, and celebrated. It was in Jerusalem that God dwelt in security, comfort, peace, and safety.

In the New Testament, there are references to the New Jerusalem — the new place of comfort, rest, and peace. The new home, the kingdom prepared by God in Jesus Christ. The New Jerusalem is God's eternal kingdom — the place we call heaven. It is the eternal dwelling place of God. The home we all journey toward, the hope of the future. It is the secure place where we are welcomed at our death, a place of comfort in grief, a place of health in sickness, a place of hope in hopelessness, a place of life in death.

Our sister now completed her journey. She now rests from all her labors, trials, and hardships of this life. And there she has found joy and peace that surpasses all that she ever experienced on earth — even in the best times of her life.

But you and I, we still travel our road of life. We still are on our journey in life. The Gospel writer, Luke, tells us something about his faith as he tells the story of the two men walking along the road to Emmaus. These two disciples were desperate, despondent, disillusioned, and discouraged. Their Lord had died and he was nowhere to be found — they could not even see his body. So they were traveling — fleeing, really — from the pain of the day he died. They hurt. They could not find him, so they moved on in their journey of life.

But as they walked, their Risen Lord came and walked with them. They talked and shared. And as Jesus asked innocent questions, they were allowed to share their hurt and pain, their confusion and distress. And in the process of their sharing, their conversation, and specifically in the sharing of a meal, these disciples recognized the Lord. He is Risen, he is Risen indeed! Now they have found new hope, new meaning, new direction in their journey of life and faith.

My friends, today in this funeral service, we share our journey of life and faith. We, like the disciples, walk together sharing our moments of doubt, and our moments of faith. We walk as the wondering, hoping, hurt, confused, and discouraged.

But our Lord walks with us. He is present with us. He is sharing our journey and life with us, bringing us hope and new faith. Renewing us with his promises, of forgiveness, love, eternal life, a New Jerusalem, wherein all believers find eternal home in Christ.

Our sister has now passed from this life through the gate of death to her eternal home. There she may find the peace and glory of the Kingdom of God. We walk yet along our journey. We walk by faith. And we walk with the Risen Savior, in whom we have the hope and the promise that all believers, though they die, yet shall they have life — new life, abundant life, eternal life. Thanks be to God for this hope.

And thanks be to God for his promises and the witness of his followers, of the gift of our sister's life, for our eternal home. And thanks be to God for his love and mercy as we continue along the journey of our life, trusting in the hope of eternal life. Amen

Hope In Christ

Isaiah 26:6-9
1 Corinthians 20-28
Mark 15:33-39; 16:1-6

One of the hardest funerals to preside over is the funeral for one who is of questionable character. And yet, in these situations, we have a unique opportunity to proclaim the pure message of the hope that a Christian has in the Risen Lord. This sermon has proven to be well received in a variety of situations.

No matter how much we prepare and think about death, when it comes we are never prepared. We are never ready. The death of one we love draws us up short, and catches us off guard. It stops us in mid-stride because we have again to confront our own immortality. We have to look into our faith and seek after the deeper meanings of hope in our lives. In short, it causes us to reflect upon and evaluate our faith and what faith has to offer us.

Today we have gathered to share faith. We have gathered as friends of a special individual. We have gathered to find comfort and support. We have gathered to find hope.

At the same time we gather to do so, we also hold in honor and memory the life of our friend. It is important to share the memories of his life with us and to cultivate the common memory of his life among us. And as we do, we praise and thank God that we had the opportunity and the privilege to share his life, to have these memories to share, and to remember his expressions of love. The gift of life is very precious and special so we can only thank God that he blessed us by placing our friend in our midst, that he blessed us by letting us share this life.

In sharing these memories, we also do much in sharing faith. For in sharing memories, we also share that portion of our life that gives us meaning and hope in the middle of our feelings of loss and grief. We share what gives us hope in the middle of a sense of hopelessness.

Over the centuries, people have shared their faith. They have shared it in words rich in imagery. They have shared it in literal language, and in picture language. They have shared it even in the words of scripture just read, which is simply a piece of faith of people of ages ago.

The center of their faith rests in the life, death, and resurrection of our Lord, Jesus Christ. The center of faith is found in this central event of Good News which makes all else have meaning and purpose. This is the only place where we can find eternal hope. This is the only place where we can find death conquered with life. This is the only message of hope that can endure.

The writer of the Gospel of Mark reports Jesus' life and death. He uses vivid words to make it perfectly clear for his readers that Jesus really died. That God's Son really went to the cross to die for the sins of humankind. But he is also clear that the story did not end there. That God's love didn't stop with death. Rather death was overcome. Death was defeated. Life was victorious. Life that is eternal, everlasting. Life that is there by faith for all believers. Life that will blossom as God raises up the dead, so that death becomes to the believer, not the end of life, but the beginning of life — new life — eternal life — abundant life — life that is far more than we can expect on this earth.

Paul in his letter to the Corinthians provides another picture of God's love. He gives us another view of the victory of God over death. Paul's confidence is really the core of the Gospel message. It is the core of our hope. The life of every Christian is to be identical to the life of Jesus. Life shall triumph over death even as Jesus, the Son of God, rose from the dead. In death, God's people are free from all the bonds and constraints of earth. All God's people are free to live new and eternal lives in the kingom of God.

Isaiah, hundreds of years earlier — provided us with another image of eternal life — the image of a lavish, joyous family feast wherein God will wipe away all tears, and all will live in love and joy.

Isaiah, Paul, and Mark couldn't see the future any more clearly than we. They, nevertheless, placed their trust, faith, and hope in a loving and kind God.

We have gathered today to thank God for the life of a loved one and to share the hope we have in Jesus Christ — God's own Son, who lived, died, and rose again by the power and grace of God. By faith, all who believe, share the same victory — victory over death and the resurrection to eternal life.

That is the faith we share. That is the hope that sustains us as we are drawn up short by death. Thanks be to God for life, and the victory won for us in the resurrection to eternal life. Thanks be to God. Amen.

For a Non-member Friend   *Mark P. Zacher*

There Is a Season

Ecclesiastes 3:1-8
Romans 8:31-35, 37-39
John 5:24-29

This sermon was preached at the funeral of a woman,
sixty years of age, who died very suddenly and unex-
pectedly.

She was not a member of my — or any — congrega-
tion, but was the mother of my next-door-neighbor.

It seemed that in the last four years or so this family
had experienced one tragedy after another. I was asked
by my next-door-neighbor to conduct the service.

For Mrs. _____, for _____, there were different
times, different seasons in her life. There was time to be a sister;
a sister to _____ and to _____ and to _____
and to _____; a sister loved and cared for. There was time
to be a wife, a beloved wife of _____. A time to build a life
together. A time to be a husband and a wife for forty-three years.
There was time to be a mother; a loving, caring mother to
_____ and to _____ and to _____ and to
_____. A time to be loving and to care and to teach; a time
to be a mother. There was time to be a grandmother, full of energy
and love and life. There was a time to be a friend, loyal and

94

concerned. As our lesson stated, *"For everything there is a season, and time for every matter under heaven . . ."* We know that that was true for _____.

But now there has come a time which we really do not understand. It just does not seem like this is the right time for death. It just does not seem like this is the right time to lose _____; to lose a beloved wife, a faithful mother, a sister, a friend. It just does not seem like this is the time or the season for this to occur. It is too sudden, too shocking, too tragic, too frightening, too unexpected, too unknown. It may seem to some of you that time-after-time this family has suffered; suffered pain and struggle and loss and grief. Perhaps in our grief and sorrow, we wonder whether there is a right time, for we cannot understand death. We cannot understand this time or this season. We cannot understand this loss. We cannot understand death; the death of a loved one, the death of our wife and mother and sister and grandmother and friend, the death of _____. We cannot understand death, even our own deaths. We cannot understand.

We gather here today, to worship God, not in order that we may find answers to our questions or that we will understand, for we may never understand the time of death. But rather, we gather here in worship to hear a message of good news, a message of hope, a message of promise, and a message of love. For there is another time. There is a time for God's salvation. There is a time for new life and resurrection. There is a time for love and for hope and for joy. In the Gospel lesson we read records Jesus' own words as he said to all of us, *"Truly, truly, I say to you, the hour is coming, and now is when the dead will hear the voice of the son of God, and those who hear will live."* Death is not a time of defeat or separation. It is not the end, the end of our season, of time with our wife and mother and sister. Rather, even in death, there is a time for hope and promise. There is for _____, and for you and me, resurrection and new life.

No, we cannot understand this time of death. For us it makes no sense. For us it is frightening and tragic. But, we have the promise and the assurance of God that this time of death is not the end. There will be a time for life and for love. _____ will rise to new life. We have God's promise. *For everything there is a season, and time for every matter under heaven . . ."*

Amen

Index of Contributors

O. Garfield Beckstrand II is pastor emeritus of Trinity Lutheran Church, Rockford, Illinois, presently serving on the Board of Pensions, LCA. He lives in Gettysburg, Pennsylvania.

Barbara Brokhoff is Evangelist for the Florida Conference, the United Methodist Church. Her residence alternates between Clearwater, Florida and Cashiers, North Carolina.

James G. Cobb is senior pastor of Trinity Lutheran Church (LCA), Grand Rapids, Michigan.

R. Blaine Detrick is a retired United Methodist pastor presently living in Egg Harbor, New Jersey.

W. George Easson is a retired pastor presently living in Las Cruces, New Mexico.

C. David Godshall is pastor of Saint Stephen's Lutheran Church (LCA), Allentown, Pennsylvania.

Charles L. Koester is pastor of Holy Trinity Lutheran Church (LCA), West Allis, Wisconsin.

Ronald J. Lavin is senior pastor of Our Saviour's Lutheran Church (LCA), Tucson, Arizona.

Alan R. Lindberg is pastor of St. John's Lutheran Church (LCA), West Milwaukee, Wisconsin.

Tom O. Miller is pastor of First Lutheran Church (LCA), Rush City, Minnesota.

Robert Noblett is pastor of First Baptist Church (ABC), Carbondale, Illinois.

Carl B. Rife is on the staff of United Theological Seminary (UMC), Dayton, Ohio.

Lawrence Ruegg is pastor of Faith Lutheran Church (LCA), Walworth, Wisconsin.

Daniel M. Shutters is pastor of Zion Lutheran Church (LCA), Dauphin, Pennsylvania.

Harold G. Skinner is pastor of St. John Lutheran Church (LCA), Cherryville, North Carolina.

Laurence A. Wagley is a professor at Saint Paul School of Theology (UMC), Kansas City, Missouri.

Stephen Youngdahl is pastor of Shepherd of the Hills Lutheran Church (LCA), Austin, Texas.

Mark P. Zacher is pastor of Immanuel Lutheran Church (LCA), Williamstown, Pennsylvania.